SPAIN

YVES BOTTINEAU

Translated by O. C. WARDEN

S P A I N

Cover Painting by YVES BRAYER

183 *illustrations in heliogravure*

NICHOLAS KAYE
LONDON

EB
PUBLISHED IN THE U. S. A. BY
ESSENTIAL BOOKS, INC.
FAIR LAWN,   NEW JERSEY

FIRST PUBLISHED IN ENGLISH
BY NICHOLAS KAYE LTD.,
BISHOPSGATE, LONDON E. C. 2
1956

FIRST PUBLISHED IN FRENCH BY B. ARTHAUD
PARIS AND GRENOBLE
UNDER THE TITLE :
L'ESPAGNE

PRINTED IN FRANCE

ACKNOWLEDGMENTS

Most of the photographs reproduced in this book were taken by YAN, Toulouse.

Others were taken by the following :

ANDERSON
Photographs on pages 23, 110, 111.

M. B. ARTHAUD, Paris
Photograph on page 45.

M. Michel AUDRAIN, Nantes
Photographs on pages 72, 73 bottom, 75, 76 top and bottom, 77, 78-79, 80, 81, 83, 84, 85, 98, 99, 210, 211 bottom, 226, 229, 231, 234, 235, 237, 238, 239, 242, 243 top and bottom, 244, 245, 246-247, 248, 249, 250, 251, 256, 257.

M. BERNARD, Paris
Photograph on page 71.

M. BOUDOT-LAMOTTE, Paris
Photograph on page 70.

M. CATALA-ROCA, Barcelona
Photographs on pages 11 top, 50, 108, 266.

Herr GRABER, Herrliberg
Photographs on pages 62, 63.

Mlle Henriette GRINDAT, Lausanne
Photograph on page 186.

M. Marcel ICHAC, Paris
Photographs on pages 230, 232, 268, 269.

M. MAINBOURG, Paris
Photograph on page 196.

M. MARMOUNIER, Aix-les-Bains
Photographs on pages 135, 260.

M. MOLLY, Paris
Photographs on pages 22, 26, 112, 113.

MUSÉE DE L'HOMME, Paris
Photograph on page 265.

M. André OSTIER, Paris
Photograph on page 66.

M. J. OSTIER, Paris
Photographs on pages 41 bottom, 61.

M. Philippe POTTIER, Paris
Photographs on pages 240, 253.

M. ROUCHON, Paris
Photographs on page 243 top.

M. SAINSAULIEU, Paris
Photograph on page 208.

Editions Pierre TISNÉ, Paris
Photograph on page 165.

M. Georges VIOLLON, Paris
Photograph on page 159.

CONTENTS

TO MY WIFE

TOLEDO. SALVADOR CHURCH.

PENISCOLA. THE CASTLE.

INTRODUCTION

COMPRISING four fifths of the Iberian Peninsula
at the south-west tip of Europe, Spain is
apparently isolated by the lofty range of the
Pyrenees — so difficult to cross, by the Atlantic
and the Mediterranean. In point of fact, it was
with Portugal, from which no natural barrier

SAGUNTO. IBERIAN SCULPTURE.

GRANADA. GARDENS OF THE GENERALIFE. THE WATER WALK.

THE GUADARRAMA PASS.

separates it, that the fewest intellectual and artistic exchanges took place and that the political union established by Philip II proved to be impossible. On the French side, the passes in the heart of the mountains and the passages at each end did not prevent armies from crossing the frontier and sufficed to ensure all sorts of contacts. By reason of its very dimensions (only eight miles wide) the Strait of Gibraltar could not protect the country against assailants from Africa. As for the long seaboards, the eastern one

13

A LEVANT FISHERMAN.

stretches along the most civilized of all basins, and the other, in the north, and to a smaller extent in the south, lies along an ocean that was to be transformed by great discoveries.

The peninsula is essentially composed of an immense central tableland, surrounded by three depressions and two lofty mountain ranges.

This tableland is the Meseta, with an average altitude of 2165 feet; it is composed of ancient soils that were affected by the Hercynian flexure.

IN GRANADA.

THE RAMPARTS OF AVILA.

Its edges rise considerably in the north in the Cantabrian Mountains, in the north-east and east in the Iberian Range ; they gradually slope down in the Sierra Morena in the south and above all in the terraces of Galicia and Portugal in the west. The Sierra of Gredos and that of Guadarrama divide the tableland into Old Castile, in the north — the land of castles whence the religious movement against the Infidels sprang — and into New Castile, in the south — the part that was reconquered. To the west lies Spanish Estremadura.

The three depressions are tertiary basins, only two of which concern Spain : north-west of the Meseta, the basin of the Ebro forms Aragon ; to the south-west, that of the Guadalquivir forms Andalusia. The third one is Portuguese Estremadura.

The two lofty ranges are flexures, likewise tertiary, which run up against the edges of the central tableland and form two mountain masses : north of the Ebro the Pyrenees, south of the Guadalquivir, the Sierra Nevada or Betic Cordillera.

The latter has the highest summit (11321 feet) before the Pyrenees (Aneto Peak 11152 feet, the Lost Mountain 10995 feet. Then the Cantabrian Mountains which reach a height of 8744 feet in the Peaks of Europe ; in the Iberian Range, the Sierra del Moncayo (7599 feet) ; in the interior of the Meseta, that of Gredos (8371 feet), that of Guadarrama (7891 feet), that of Guadalupe between New Castile and Estremadura (5112 feet). The highest point of the Sierra Morena is not more than 4625 feet. The southern part of the tableland is appreciably lower than the northern. In the depressions we descend abruptly to an altitude of 820 feet in the trench of the Ebro and to 328 feet in that of the Guadalquivir.

The Balearic Isles, which prolong the Betic Cordillera in the north as the Rif prolongs it in the south, reach their highest point at 5151 feet.

The climate of the Meseta is severe and extreme. Snow and wind rage there in winter. In summer the heat is oppressive and the landscapes sun-drenched. The climate of the Ebro basin is almost as severe. In the north and north-west, along the Atlantic coast, the salutary influence of the Gulf-Stream is felt ; there is plenty of rain and summer and winter are temperate. Thanks to the sea, the shores of Andalusia enjoy an extremely mild climate ; the basin of the Guadalquivir has more distinct seasons. But the Mediterranean seaboard surpasses the other regions with its long summers, delightful spring-time and mild winters.

Spain, where there are almost no lakes, does not have the conditions necessary for the existence of rivers at once mighty and useful. The mountains are situated on the periphery of the country, it seldom rains and the soil is often impermeable ; so the rivers flow irregularly, although they may reach the coast laden with alluvial deposits and form deltas ; their swiftly flowing waters are swept along to sharply changing altitudes and hollow out the relief they so greatly modify in all sorts of ways.

Only coastal rivers flow into the Atlantic in the north and west as far as the Portuguese frontier; the Miño separates Galicia from Portugal. Likewise on the Atlantic coast, but farther south, flow the Duero and the Tagus, which flow into the sea beyond the Spanish border, and the Guadiana which constitutes the frontier near the sea : they are tableland rivers which have to make their way across the western edges of the Meseta.

The Guadalquivir, which falls into the ocean east of the Guadiana, is quite different : the vital channel of communications in Andalusia, seventy-five miles of it are navigable; thanks to it, Seville is a great port and was able to play an essential part in trade with the Spanish colonies in America.

The delta of the Ebro runs out into the Mediterranean; its flow is that of a steppe river.

The rocky Atlantic coast is deeply indented : the soil has settled down in the spots which offered the least resistance, bringing out the difference between the level of the coastal mountains which refused to be submerged and that of the first soil covered by the sea. A particularity of Galicia is the presence of *rias*; they are the ancient valleys that the slow submersion of the mountains transformed into bays of multifarious shapes, similar to Norwegian *fjords*. The most beautiful and famous one is that of Vigo : between the green hills, the sea traces blue arabesques on the land.

The coast of Andalusia is flat and sandy as far as Gibraltar. Just before its mouth, the Guadalquivir flows through stretches of mire and clay, and canals called the *Marismas ;* there it divides into several branches. Sometimes the coast becomes rocky and in such a spot we find the strange peninsula of Cadiz.

The Mediterranean shore is composed of a succession of graceful curves. The different mountain ranges form admirable landscapes on reaching the seaboard. The coastal rivers have created little alluvial plains. To the east dunes and, off shore, bars shelter lagoons such as the Albuferas of Valencia and the Mar Menor near Cartagena. Even in ancient times the sub-soil proved to be rich; today copper is mined in the region of Huelva, and coal in Asturias, as well as lead, silver and iron.

The vegetation varies according to the humidity of the climate and thus helps to divide Spain into a certain number of natural regions. Galicia and the Cantabrian shore are very green. On the Meseta there are wheat fields in Old Castile and true steppes in New Castile. Andalusia with its warm and varied climate is extremely fertile; its coast reminds us of Africa. The east, which enjoys a Mediterranean climate on its seaboard, tends towards steppes inland and owes part of its prosperity to the irrigation of the *huertas*. Aragon and Catalonia are influenced by the sea and the mountains.

Long centuries of history have emphasized the divisions proposed by nature. The paintings in the caves at Altamira and near Albacete acquaint us with the arduous existence of the first inhabitants of the peninsula.

SEVILLE CATHEDRAL. THE TOMB OF CHRISTOPHER COLUMBUS.

But we know little about their origins and just as little about those whom Strabo was later to call Celts and Iberians. The Basques of the present day descend from them.

The Phoenicians set up trading-posts on sites which reminded them of Tyre — for instance, in Cadiz. Their influence left mementoes which are particularly worthy of note on the little island of Ibiza, one of the Balearic Isles.

The Greeks founded Ampurias and had a much greater influence on Iberian art and civilization.

First called over by the Phoenicians, the Carthaginians, after losing Sicily, sought to compensate this surrender by the conquest of what is now Andalusia, the foundation of Cartagena (Carthago Nova), and the capture of Salamanca and Toro. They had promised Rome not to go beyond the Ebro : so when Hannibal took Sagunto (219 B. C.) after a memorable siege, the Second Punic war broke out. Hannibal left Spain, making for Italy. The Romans rushed in to conquer the Peninsula. Publius Cornelius Scipio took Cartagena and Cadiz and founded Italica (206 B. C.) not far from our Seville.

But the legions had to struggle for many a long year to make the peninsula Roman territory. The resistance of a humble shepherd, Viriatus, who had become a war-leader, only came to an end in 139 B. C. Scipio Aemilianus had to come in person to take besieged Numantia which only surrendered after a bitter resistance which won it lasting fame (133 B. C.). Sertorius's revolt is more interesting. A military tribune in Spain, a member of Marius's party, he was dismissed by the governor appointed by Sylla, and hailed as leader by the native population. When Pompey tried to reduce him, he only succeeded through the treachery of one of Sylla's lieutenants, Perpenna, who killed him during a banquet. But in his way Sertorius had tried to Romanize the inhabitants under his orders and authority.

Caesar, who conquered Pompey's sons at Munda (45 B. C.) doubtless remembered this example. The conquest was only completed in 19 B. C. Divided into provinces, Spain was endowed with the language and legislation of Rome. An immense network of roads was laid out, magnificent cities built : Saragossa *(Caesarea Augusta)*, Merida *(Augusta Emerita)*, and aqueducts were erected. Their admirable ruins bear witness to the fact that Rome not only took care to practise a policy of prestige but also watched over the actual needs of the inhabitants. But the country took an active part in the life of the Empire. It was not in vain that the future Augustus sojourned at Tarragona and Agrippa at Merida. Italica was the birth-place of Trajan, Hadrian and Theodosius, and Cordoba that of the two Senecas and, as early as Caesar's day, of Lucan.

Roman domination was undoubtedly too closely confined to cities and the zones of communications to instil the notion of the State into the inhabitants. In any case, Theodosius's death in 395 and the cleavage of the Empire into two separate worlds — one with Byzantium for its capital, the other Rome — heralded the arrival of hordes of Barbarians who swept through Spain where Christianity, which had already been introduced, gloried in its many martyrs. The peninsula played an important part in the Church, participating in Councils and giving it a Pope in the person of Damasus, but also a heretic in that of Priscillian. So it was already possible to recognize a few tendencies of the national temperament which were to become more explicit in the following centuries.

In 409 the Suevi and Vandals crossed the Pyrenees ; the latter settled in Baetica — that the Arabs were to call Andalusia. In their turn, the Goths drove back the other Barbarians and organized a huge State which spread from the Pillars of Hercules to the Loire during Euric's reign. But they were Arians and a rapacious war-leader, Clovis, a Frank, backed by the bishops of Catholic Gaul, vanquished King Alaric II the Goth at Vouillé in 507 ; after the latter's death, the monarchy subsisted in Spain, and Toledo, promoted to the rank of capital, was the seat of a brilliant court. Athanagild married his daughters to Frankish princes : Galswinthe to Chilperic, and the famous Brunhild to Sigebert. For some time Baetica was under the domination of Byzantium, as a result of internal dissension in the Visigothic Kingdom. But the religious problem became acute when the heir to the throne, Hermenegild, was converted to Catholicism by the bishop of Seville, Leander, Isidorus's brother — two great names in the Church and humanities of that period. The prince was martyred (585). His brother, King Reccared, was converted in his turn two years afterwards and his was the happiest reign of all the Visigothic sovereigns.

The domestic struggles in which his successors were involved coincided with the westward march of Islam along the Mediterranean shores. In 683, the Arabs were in Morocco. In 711 Tarik the Berber, Moussa Ibn Nacer's lieutenant, crossed the strait and landed on the spot since called " Djebel Tarik " (Gibraltar). The troops of the last Gothic king, Roderic, were beaten in the Battle of the Guadalete (July 19). The sovereign's power collapsed. The kingdom of which he was the last ruler had only afforded its inhabitants the rather unedifying example of a civilization which was certainly very brilliant but also superficial. And Spain, after so many centuries during which conquerors had succeeded one another, had been taught intellectual and artistic lessons but it still had only a vague idea of unity or government : in other words, of a real State.

While the sway of the Arabs was spreading over the peninsula and was only stopped in Gaul itself by Charles Martel at Poitiers (732), a handful of nobles, led by the Romanized Goth Pelayo or Pelage, put up a vigorous resistance to the Moslem invaders in Asturias and won a signal victory at Covadonga (718). This success was the first of a centuries-long struggle which came to an end with the capture of Granada in 1492. But the name of Covadonga is significant of even more : the strength of religious belief and, equally powerful, the reflex of independence which made use of the surface of the country, and the shelter which the mountains afforded the invaded. Thus, in the very origin of the Reconquest that was to forge its unity, Spain did not escape either from the exigencies of its soil or from its individualism, the characteristic feature of its national soul.

Up to the end of the fifteenth century, the Moslems in the south and

THE ESCURIAL. DETAIL OF THE DREAM OF PHILIP II, BY EL GRECO.

the Christian kingdoms in the north shared the peninsula. The Reconquest, which takes on an imposing turn as we look back at it across the centuries, but was actually a very human medley of greatness and quite natural compromises, appeared as an immense tidal wave which flowed forth from Asturias and Leon and finally swallowed up the Infidels completely. But during the first centuries there was a slow and uncertain movement like the ebb and flow of the tide, which can easily be explained. Moslem Spain knew four powerful dynasties : the Omeyades, the Almoravides, the Almohades, the Nasrides, that only succeeded one another after troubled interludes. Confronting them, the Christian princes only united temporarily

MADRID. THE SAN FERNANDO ACADEMY. PIETA, BY MORALES.

and there was much internal discord within the States ; the number of kingdoms was only reduced through marriages and they sometimes juxtaposed the regions instead of giving them a common soul.

In the east, the Omeyades had been overthrown by the Abassides in 750. A member of the fallen family, Abd Er Rhaman, took refuge in North Africa and passed over into Spain ; he proclaimed himself an independent Emir (756), and Cordoba became the capital of a Moslem State and remained so for several centuries. An oriental and Islamic civilization was about to bloom on the Hispanic and Christian foundations ; it was to influence northern Spain and leave an undying mark on the national character.

It was under Abd Er Rhaman III (912-961), who proclaimed himself Caliph in 929, and especially under Hachem II (961-976) that the art and prosperity of Moslem Andalusia reached their zenith. After Hachem's death, the vizier El Mansour won the victory of Calatanazor. But the same phenomenon that was to take place for each dynasty occurred, and the Omeyades fell from power, the Caliphate disappeared in the anarchy and its territory was parcelled out among some twenty petty princes, the kings of Taïfas. Against the magnificent and powerful Omeyades, the Christian peninsula could only present divided forces. The Asturian kings, successors of Pelayo, transferred their capital to Leon which gave its name to the new kingdom.

In the middle of the eleventh century, four states shared the north of Spain : the County of Barcelona, Aragon, Navarre and Castile. In 1035 Ferdinand I had taken the title of King of Castile and annexed Leon by marriage — but the union was only to become definitive under Ferdinand III (St. Ferdinand).

In 1137 Ramon Berenguer IV, Count of Barcelona, ensured the union of Catalonia and Aragon by marrying a princess of that country.

Thus two sovereigns seemed to be destined to share most of the Christian territories : the ruler of Castile, lying in the heart of the peninsula, and consequently the most qualified to unite the States, and the ruler of Aragon, more disposed to fulfil a Mediterranean destiny.

The constant support of the Papacy, the backing of great French noble families connected to the Spanish kings through intermarriage, the foundation of the Military Orders of Santiago, Alcantara (1156) and Calatrava (1158), ensured the success of the Reconquest, considered as a Crusade long before the expeditions to the Holy Land. Not only the Popes but also the Abbots of Cluny sent knights to fight beyond the Pyrenees.

Ferdinand I recaptured many towns held by of the kings of Taïfas. At the time of the Cid's heroic deeds, Alfonso VI took Toledo (1085) and made it his capital, and founded Portugal in 1094 for Henry of Burgundy. But the petty Moslem princes appealed to their co-religionists in North Africa. The Almoravides, who had come from Senegal and had already conquered Morocco, landed in Andalusia; they vanquished the Christian king at Uclès (1108) and, substituting their domination for that of the minor Moslem princes, reigned over an empire which spread on both sides of Gibraltar.

In their turn, they were replaced by the Almohades who beat Alfonso VIII of Castile at Alarcos (1195).

This new resurgence of Islam, supplied by the African tribes, roused Christian Europe and it was only checked in 1212 at Las Navas de Tolosa — one of the most glorious victories in Spanish history.

Two great kings then reigned, one over Aragon — Jaime I (1213-1276), who took the Balearic Isles; the other over Castile — St. Ferdinand, a cousin of St. Louis of France (1217-1252). Thanks to the latter, the Reconquest made a great stride forward. He took Ubeda, Cordoba (1236), Murcia (1241), and, after a long siege, Seville (1248). It meant the downfall of the Almohades. But the Nasrides, their former auxiliaries, declared their independence and, taking advantage of the discord in Christian Spain after the death of the two great sovereigns, continued to exert Moslem domination in Granada until the end of the fifteenth century.

The troubles which stirred up Aragon and Castile — one has but to think of the death of Peter the Cruel (1350-1369), killed by his brother Henry of Transtamare in Duguesclin's tent — only came to an end with the marriage of Ferdinand, the heir to the first kingdom, and Isabella, the heir to the second one (1469). They reigned jointly — they were the Catholic Kings — over Castile from 1474 and over Aragon from 1479.

There then began a period of extraordinary splendour for Spain. From the political point of view, it lasted until the end of Philip II's reign; from the literary and artistic point of view, until the end of the seventeenth century.

The very same year, 1492, witnessed the capture of Granada and the discovery of America by Christopher Columbus — the beginning of a series of explorations and conquests which were to give the Spanish kings half the world. It also witnessed the expulsion of the Jews, which produced a disastrous effect on the economy of the country.

Once the Moors were driven out and the union of the States accomplished through one marriage, unity had still to be achieved. The Catholic religion had been the underlying spirit of the Reconquest; it remained the common faith that was to be that of all Spaniards; this explains the expulsion of the Jews and the Inquisition — the undeniable severity of the latter perhaps spared the peninsula religious wars like those in France, and a recent example has shown us how atrocious such struggles can be in Spain.

The country still bears the stamp of the way in which its unification was brought about. The kingdoms joined together but did not merge: the independence of each one was succeeded by the particularism which

MADRID. THE PRADO. DETAIL FROM THE NAKED MAJA BY GOYA.

is evident in their fondness for *fueros*, or local privileges. Precisely because of the importance of religion in their national history, religious intolerance was to lead to a fanaticism prejudicial to the country's economic system — the most striking example is the expulsion of the Moors under Philip III.

To the eccentric tendencies of Catalonia, Aragon added the dynastic aspirations of her princes towards Naples. Gonzalve of Cordoba, the 'Gran Capitan' saved Ferdinand's possessions in Southern Italy in the struggle with France.

The marriage of Joanna, the Catholic Sovereigns' daughter, to Philip the Handsome, son of the Emperor Maximilian and Mary of Burgundy, gave promise of additional territories to Spain — but involved her in the complications of continental politics where she inevitably clashed with France, who was uneasy about her excessive power.

26

When Isabella died in 1504 before Ferdinand, who lived on until 1516, Spain found herself faced with several alternatives : should she turn towards Africa as the great queen had requested in her will ; should she devote herself to her overseas empire ; should she become a Mediterranean and European power ; should she forge her unity by doing away with the particularism of the ancient kingdoms ? Each of these solutions ensured her grandeur — she chose them all, and in the overwhelming effort she made — despite all the gold she received from America — she proved sublime. The Burgundian heritage — through the luck of inheritances — gave Spain a predominant position in Europe ; she proved to be more than worthy of it...

Unfortunately, Joanna, a victim of her heredity and morbid jealousy, went mad and Philip the Handsome died before his time (1506).

Their son Charles, who had been brought up in Flanders, arrived in Spain in 1517, after Cardinal Cisneros had ensured the regency. He reigned not only over Spain but also over Sardinia, Sicily, Naples, Roussillon, Flanders and the territories in the New World. Elected emperor in 1520, Charles V became one of the most powerful monarchs known to history.

Francis I, Charles's unhappy rival for the title of Emperor, could not accept the maintenance of a sovereignty which completely encircled his States. Besides, the possessor of the larger part of Europe and the New World allowed himself to be hypnotized by a side-issue ; he laid claim to Burgundy as his father's ancestral land. When the birth of Protestantism had divided Christendom, Spain was obliged to add two other undertakings to her own problems : the impossible recapture of Burgundy, which Francis I, after his release from the Alcazar in Madrid where Charles had kept him prisoner after the battle of Pavia, took care not to surrender to him ; the upholding of the Catholic religion throughout Europe.

The resources of Mexico conquered by Cortez, of Peru conquered by Pizarro, of all the West Indies and the Philippines, were too often spent on undertakings which had little to do with the peninsula itself.

Charles V, victorious over the Protestants at Mühlberg (1547), was not able to break down the resistance of France. Finally, worn out by incessant struggles, he rid himself of the power which had been heaped upon him. His brother Ferdinand received the Empire and the hereditary possessions of the Hapsburgs ; he gave Spain, Italy, Flanders and America to his son Philip.

Philip II (1555-1598), a convinced Spaniard, fought against the particularism which had already stirred up the peninsula during his father's reign. He made his kingdom the champion of the Catholic religion, at the same time pursuing a policy of European hegemony. But he broke down the resistance neither of France nor of the Low Countries, alienated by a savage repression. The victory of Saint-Quentin (1557) was rendered void by the capture of Calais, taken from the English and his second wife,

Mary Tudor. At the end of the century, the agitation of the League finally prevented the king from putting a stop to the accession of Henry IV to the throne of France. He had to separate the indomitable Low Countries : the Protestant United Provinces became independent, Catholic Flanders remained under the sway of Spain.

Elizabeth's heretical England, threatened by the Invincible Armada, was saved by the storm which scattered the vessels (1588). The failure was evident — and Spain, glorious though she might be, was exhausted.

At all events, the victory of Lepanto (October 7, 1571) had shed a rare glory on the kingdom. Don Juan of Austria, Charles V's illegitimate son, routed the fleet of Islam.

In 1581, as the Portuguese dynasty had become extinct, Philip II became king of Portugal. His desire to reign over the whole peninsula had led him to commit a fatal mistake. Portugal was an Atlantic country, looking seawards ; henceforth her only concern was to throw off the yoke, and she was to harbour a lasting resentment against her neighbour for her period of bondage.

Neither Philip III (1598-1621) nor Philip IV (1621-1665) had the ability to realize the true destiny of their nation and to reform its administration. They did not find the ministers who might have deputized for them — and Olivarès, the most gifted of them all, had to contend with Richelieu. At Rocroi (1643), the structure of greatness and glory which had been handed down to them received a death blow from which it was never to recover. France forced on Philip IV, in the treaty of the Pyrenees (1659), the surrender of Roussillon and the marriage of Louis XIV to Philip's daughter Maria-Theresa. The Bourbons now held first place in Europe.

Charles II, born of a valetudinary father, dragged out a long sickly existence. The problem of his succession which was unceasingly debated was solved by Spain herself who considered powerful Louis XIV to be far more fitted to maintain the integrity of the kingdoms than the weak emperor. This hope was disappointed. The treaties of Utrecht deprived Philip V of Flanders and Italy.

The Bourbons — Philip V (1700-1746), Ferdinand VI (1746-1759), Charles III (1759-1788), the most capable of them all — devoted their efforts to the administrative reorganization of the country and gave free rein to excellent ministers like Patino, La Ensenada, Aranda. The establishment of Spanish princes in Naples and Parma compensated the losses of the War of the Spanish Succession, and the development of the West Indies — it would have been even more important without the yearning to reconquer the lost territories — made the eighteenth century a great period of colonial expansion for Spain.

Charles IV, dominated by Queen Maria-Louisa and Godoy, most certainly did not do his duty to his country and his misfortune opposed him to Napoleon. The unwarrantable intervention of the Emperor in the

VALENCIA MUSEUM. SELF-PORTRAIT, BY VELASQUEZ.

peninsula brought about the heroic reactions of the War of Independence, marked by unatonable atrocities on both sides.

Ferdinand VII disappointed the liberals' hopes and when he died left his throne to his daughter, Isabella II, to the detriment of his brother Don Carlos. The absolutists sided with the prince, the liberals with the

PENITENTS OF SEVILLE.

THE ESCURIAL. CHRIST OF THE GOOD DEATH.

queen. The kingdom, repudiated by its American colonies, which had proclaimed their independence, was divided by long civil wars. It was only during the reign of Alfonso XII (1874-1885) that the country grew calm once again. Maria-Christina's regency was particularly happy for the homeland. But the war with the United States resulted in the loss of all that remained of the overseas empire (1898) : Cuba, Porto-Rico, Guam and the Philippines.

Alfonso XIII was forced to abdicate in 1931. The Republic was immediately caught up in the throes of a civil war (1936-39) from which the country has not yet recovered.

Among the national arts of Europe, that of Spain is one of the most original and offers the most contrasts — it is also the one which most readily fluctuates between two excesses.

It has been profoundly affected by foreign influences : the Phoenicians, Greece and Rome, Byzantium, Romanesque and Gothic France, the Flemish painters, Renaissance Italy, eighteenth-century France. Open to so many currents, apparently buried under manifold alluvia, it has only become a more authentic expression of the national soul. It has kept but forms and means of expression and coloured them with the genius of the race.

The East and West are both set against each other and mingled in Spanish art. It will try to combine both lessons. From Islam it borrows a horror of empty space in decoration, the infinite repetition of identical motifs, the use of brick... Is not Mozarabic art, which is pre-eminently a national art, Christian in its aim but Moslem in its technique and even in its inspiration ? Spain will try in vain to suppress the memory of Islamic civilization — the work of centuries cannot be destroyed. If the cathedrals and churches built on the sites of mosques had been torn down when the Moors were driven out of Spain, how many sanctuaries would have been left to worship the true God ?

Spanish art is so concerned with realism and its rendering that it uses human skin and hair. Yet it attains serenity and, with Velazquez, reaches an impassibility which is perhaps unrivalled in the history of painting.

It delights in detailed and gory martyrdoms : the executioner cuts off breasts and carefully slices off strips of flesh. But it is sometimes steeped in a mystical atmosphere — and in a piety which may become sickly. These contrasts are only one of the aspects of a universal canon of art, that of the fluctuation between classical reserve and baroque overloading. The originality of Spanish art consists in carrying them out to the very extreme : flowery Gothic and chased *plateresco*, then the severe Escurial, the extravagant and sometimes fascinating style of the Churriguera, and last of all, neo-classicism.

During our trip we shall visit the principal museums. Here we can only give the general lines of the evolution to which they bear witness.

The most distant ages have handed down to us works of arts which give proof of the summits reached by their art : prehistory, the grottoes of Altamira the Iberian period, the Lady of Elche, so mysteriously noble [1].

Rome furnished the manifold example of its monumental grandeur, with its aqueducts, amphitheatres, enceintes and bridges whose beauty consists in corresponding precisely to their function : the architects who designed them seem to have breathed an air as all-embracing as the Empire. Over how many rivers have the ancient arches of a *Puente Romano* afforded a passage for centuries ?

Thanks to the Visigothic kings, Spain knew the splendour of the goldsmith's art of the Middle Ages. The Treasure of Guarrazzar, discovered near Toledo in the last century (1858 and 1860) surprises one by its astonishing sumptuousness : crowns, crosses, pendants and chains [2].

Thanks to Abd Er Rhaman who began to build the great mosque of Cordoba (785), Moslem Andalusia early enjoyed a brilliant civilization which could not help attracting the rest of the peninsula. Abd Er Rhaman III dedicated the residence of Medinat az Zhara near the capital of his States to his favourite.

In the Christian States the Mozarabic civilization, already influenced by Islamic architecture, developed in the tenth century. Its chief edifices are found in Leon, e. g. San Miguel de Escalada.

The northern half of the peninsula was soon to submit to the triumphant fascination of France. Caught between that of Islam and that of Romanesque and afterwards Gothic France, it was to work out its own art.

The knights who had come from France to fight the Infidel and above all the Cluny monks and the pilgrims of St. James brought Romanesque art into the north-west. Sculpture quickly assumed Spanish traits as is shown by the cloister of Silos and the porch of Glory of Santiago. In the north-east, Catalonia, already manifesting the particular tendencies of its temperament, developed an original Romanesque art, at first strong and archaic, then prolific in sculpture and harsh, moving primitive paintings.

Unfortunately little remains to acquaint us with the Moslem twelfth and thirteenth centuries in Spain. The elegant Giralda in Seville dates back to this period. St. Mary the White in Toledo at least proves the far-reaching scope of the Andalusian influence and, by their resemblance, the historic edifices of North Africa can furnish us with information about the art of Moslem Spain.

The fourteenth and fifteenth centuries were fruitful, brilliant and complex. In Granada the Alhambra was built ; its rooms and patios still offer daydreamers a setting more elegant than those of their most beautiful

---

(1 and 2) The Lady of Elche, shown at the Louvre before the war, and part of the Treasure of Guarrazzar acquired by the Cluny Museum are now in Madrid (the Prado, Archaelogical Museum) as a result of an exchange (1940) which has not yet been settled by France and Spain.

IN THE SEVILLE BULLRING.

PICADORS.

dreams. The Gothic art of France with its stirring cathedrals spread through the north and southwards as far as the portion of Andalusia rescued from the Infidels : Burgos, Leon, Toledo, Seville. The Arabian influence was still enormous in Mozarabic art which welcomed and assimilated the processes, decorative motifs and techniques of Islamic civilization.

The most characteristic buildings have an inimitable gusto : the Seo or Old Cathedral of Saragossa, Tordesillas, part of the Alcazar of Seville, the Transito synagogue in Toledo, the great cloister of Guadalupe. Ceramics from Andalusia took root in the east and multiplied the dishes of Manises with their metallic gleams.

In painting regional schools of early masters flourished and we shall have the opportunity to admire their retables in Castile, Catalonia, and the countryside of Valencia. The influence of Italy seems to have been inferior to that of Flanders which spread far and wide not only thanks to the genius of its artists but also to a journey Jan Van Eyck made to Spain, and to political relations. A Hispano-Flemish school was born in which the detailed and exuberant colouring of Flanders mingled with the pathos of Spain.

Despite an apparent paradox, the period of the Catholic Kings was original to a degree. It was paradoxical because foreigners took a hand in creating the most genuinely national style and public buildings. Of the architects Juan Guas and Enrique de Egas, one was born in Lyons and the other in Brussels. The sculptor Gil de Siloé hailed from Antwerp. Arabic elements mingled with the last Gothic traditions in the style of Isabella de San Juan de los Reyes at Toledo.

In the same period, the *plateresco* style (from *platero*, goldsmith) with its finely chiselled stone evoked the goldmith's delicate art. But already the sculptor Domenico Fancelli heralded the Italian influence characteristic of the Renaissance.

This influence developed in the smiling art of the period of Charles V ; its most distinguished representatives were the architects Juan Gil de Hontañon and his son Rodrigo, and Alonso de Covarrubias. Diego de Siloé, Gil's son, was both an architect and a sculptor.

The worthy Alonso Berruguete, the son of the early master Pedro, attained the most perfect expression of Spanish genius. In his sculpture even more than in his paintings, Alonso, a pupil of Michelangelo, was able to express a physiological and moral pathos which was not mere gesticulation ; his work was done at the very period when Spanish polychrome sculpture reached the standard of a universally valid art. Juan de Juni, although he was a native of France, easily lapsed into a grandiloquent style.

Alongside the official art of the Renaissance, polychrome sculpture is the representation of the depths of the country's soul ; once we have accepted it, we are subjugated forever and it remains bound up in our memories of Holy Weeks.

The huge retables rising in stages behind the altars, the *sillerias* which display their superimposed rows of carved seats in the canons' *coro* are other privileged spots where Spanish genius is most genuinely expressed. Popular art, which reflects the deep-seated inclinations of the race, plays a more important part than in France. Thanks to the many orders it placed, the influence of the Church was at least as great as that of the kings.

The Italianization of art became more pronounced under Philip II, with a more majestic and severe character ; its most perfect example is the Escurial by Juan Bautista de Toledo and Juan de Herrera. It embodies not only the art of a reign but the character of a king and a tendency of the Spanish character — the one that prompts it to cast off all superfluous decoration.

The Golden Age of Spanish civilization corresponds to the period in its political history — from the end of the sixteenth century to the end of the seventeenth — which on the other hand, was marked by a continual decline in the country's greatness.

In Toledo, El Greco had already furnished an admirable picture of the society of his day. Luis de Morales, Sanchez Cœllo, Pantoja de la Cruz gave promise of the artists who were soon to carry Spanish painting to its zenith : Francisco Ribalta in Valencia, Ribera, of Spanish descent and manner, though he lived in Naples (which moreover belonged to Spain), in Seville Herrera el Viejo and Herrera el Mozo his son, Pacheco, Velazquez's master and father-in-law, then Zurbaran (1598-1664), Murillo (1617-1682), Valdès Leal (1622-1690) — and finally, Velazquez (1599-1660), in Madrid, whose name alone overshadows all the others.

Polychrome sculpture made great strides in Castile thanks to Gregorio Fernandez (1566-1636), in Seville thanks to Montañès (1568-1649). Pedro de Mena (1628-1688), a native of Granada, was to carry on their tradition. Alonso Cano (1601-1667), at one and the same time a sculptor, painter and architect, led a stormy life and was even accused of murdering his wife.

The first half of the eighteenth century was the period of baroque art. In the field of architecture, Pedro de Ribera built monuments in Madrid which escaped the influence of the Escurial. The Churrigueras developed a heavy type of decoration which was very much criticized and long misunderstood, and its excesses were indeed open to criticism, but it was often endowed with an undeniable force. Baroque art is moreover the expression of a tendency of the national character and it was all the more affected as the Princes of the house of Bourbon called in Italians and Frenchmen and created an official art, closely akin to the international academism of the day.

The second half of the century was marked by neo-classicism, a phenomenon common to the whole of Europe.

The dazzling light of Goya's genius (1746-1828) suffused half a century of history : a painter of the happy life in his cartoons for tapestries, a fierce, veracious portrait-painter of the royal family, hallucinated visionary, or a patriot torn with anguish by the *Disasters of War*. It seems as if it were useless to try anything after such a master. The public is ill-informed about the great artists that Spain has never ceased to produce and we can only enumerate them : Vicente Lopez, an official portrait-painter (1772-1850) ; and more recently Zuloaga. At the present time Picasso and Dali prove that the violent temperament of the race needs only a favourable climate to blossom into works of art.

TOLEDO LACE.

Leaving the Basques aside because of the very particular nature of their language and customs, we may say the Spanish race is the product of a multiple fusion. Ligurians, Celts, Phoenicians, Carthaginians, Romans, Barbarians who had settled in the Empire, Arabs and Jews have blended together. Actually the traveller is more responsive to the regional differences than to the general character of the inhabitants. The Andalusian, marked by the Arab domination, is exuberant and nostalgic. The Castilian headstrong and readily mystical. The Catalan and inhabitant of the east coast, bred within sight of the sea, are drawn to trade.

The Basque willingly emigrates...

After three years of civil war, Spain was cut off from the outside world by the second World War. Once peace was re-established, the French frontier was closed. Only in recent years has the country been able to look forward to more normal economic conditions. Industry is still geographically localized in a few provinces : Catalonia (textiles), the East, the Asturias and the Basque country (iron-smelting). At Huelva the copper, silver and mercury mines bear witness to the wealth of the sub-soil — but it is still insufficiently worked for want of the necessary equipment. Thanks to the coal in the Asturias the region around Oviedo is one of the busiest spots in the peninsula. The great effort made to develop water-power is beginning to bear fruit.

But Spain is still an agricultural land : the scanty crops of Castile, the rich sweeping plains of Andalusia, covered with vines, orange and olive trees, the *huertas* of the Levant, and the pasture lands of Aragon where flocks of sheep roam here and there under the care of solitary shepherds...

THE ALCAZAR, SEVILLE. DETAIL OF A MOSAIC.

FISHERMEN AT PUERTO DE LA SELVA.

PORT LLIGAT. FISHERMEN'S HOUSES AND THE FARNERA ROCK.

CHAPTER I

CATALONIA

THE BALEARIC ISLES

ARAGON

FROM Perpignan we drive down towards Barcelona. The coast road, via the Costa Brava, hilly and picturesque, with bright colours,

AT PALMA DE MAJORCA.

41

GERONA. GENERAL VIEW.

follows the contours of the shore. At the far end of its cove Cadaquès welcomes us. In Ampurias we find memories of Greece and Rome. Palamos is built on a promontory and offers us its XIth-century Porta Ferrada.

Inland, the picturesque old districts of Gerona and its artistic treasures make a stop-over obligatory. Along the Rio Güell, a row of tall houses

GERONA. SOBREPORTAS GATE.

forms an unexpected rampart on both banks : each floor is fronted by a terrace-like balcony and the rusty brown walls of the old houses seem to be constantly soiling the snow-white linen waving in the wind.

All around the cathedral, amidst the mossy grey freestones disjointed by the invading plants, we find only steep stairs among the winding streets. Suddenly, the façade of the sanctuary looms before us at the top of a flight of steps, so wide and noble that a king in all his glory would gladly climb it ; its baroque stories with coupled columns, surmounted by a rose-window,

GERONA. SAN PEDRO DE GALLIGANS : THE CLOISTER.

RIPOLL. DETAIL OF THE FAÇADES OF THE ABBEY. (RIGHT SIDE.)

seem to have been stuck on the edifice built from the XIVth to the XVIth centuries. The right-hand tower, the only one that was built, ensures the upward surge of the mass ; the severity of the walls would be complete without the elegant decoration worthy of a palace. Inside, we are surprised by the sumptuous retable of the great altar, made of wood covered with sheets of chased silver : this work, dating from the XIVth century, is devoted to scenes from the New Testament.

How many beautiful things this Cathedral keeps in store for us ! The Romanesque galleries of the cloister, the door of the Apostles standing open on the tranquil, almost monastic-like square of the Bishop's palace, the paintings by early Catalan masters, the gold plate ! The *Cloth of Creation*, a large piece of embroidery of the late XIth or XIIth centuries shows us the history of Man from the moment when the Spirit of God breathed over the waters down to the finding of the true Cross.

The surrounding district contains other buildings raised during the Catalonian Middle Ages ; they constitute as many perfect and evocative architectural gems around the cathedral. The small Romanesque Church of *San Pedro de Galligans* has been turned into a museum. The round-headed archways of a sort of circular temple stand out against the tall

VICH CATHEDRAL. PAINTING BY JOSÉ-MARIA SERT. ST. LUKE.

BARCELONA AT NIGHT FROM GUELL PARK.

BARCELONA. IN THE HARBOUR.

buildings nearby. The Arabian baths, so poetical and mysterious, seem rather to be mozarabic and must date back to the XIIth or XIIIth centuries.

Before leaving the town and going on to Barcelona, we must stop near the Ayuntamiento and visit the diocesan museum. It houses an impressive collection of early Catalan masters. Amidst the glittering gold paint, Luis Borrassà painted the *Saint Michael* of the Cruilles retable ; the Archangel triumphing over the Devil and the Christ dying on the Cross date from the XVth century ; each of them adds a page to the sublime story of the redemption of Man which the *Cloth of the Creation* has already told us. It is Martorell who painted this seated St. Peter with a tiara on his head ; he is a leader of the Church in the Christian tradition of the day: magnificent, kind and staunch.

From Toulouse in France we may go to Barcelona by way of Puigcerda, through gripping mountain landscapes or by way of Ripoll and Vich, lying a few miles apart, where we can see two of the most sublime products of medieval art in Catalonia.

As early as 888 a temple to the Virgin was erected at Ripoll. During the following century the surrounding monastery became so important that a new church was consecrated in its turn in 977 ; that might have been considered definitive but such was not the case. Having become a religious and intellectual centre of the first magnitude in monastic Christendom of the day, the abbey witnessed the building of a new sanctuary under the abbacy of Oliva, who belonged to the family of the Counts of Cerdagne and Besalù. It was solemnly inaugurated on January 15, 1032. The famous portal we now admire dates back to the twelfth century, and the first work on the cloister was done at the same date ; the work was afterwards continued and a second storey whose style is scrupulously exact was added.

But thenceforth misfortune fell upon Ripoll. After the earthquake of February 2, 1428, the church was covered with sham Gothic vaults. The baroque period contributed a quantity of retables in questionable taste. In 1826-1830, under the pretext of restoring them, the naves were mutilated. In 1835, during the political disturbances, the monastery was sacked and looted, then utterly neglected. It was raised from its ruins and the new church was inaugurated in 1893.

We cannot fail to be moved by the portal and cloister, authentic remains of the monastery which was the Pantheon of the Counts of Barcelona. In the former the sculptors have given an interpretation of the Bible which is a true epic poem in stone. We are carried away by the harmony of the latter as we go from capital to capital discovering the multifarious characters and types of foliage.

The first masterpiece was a monastery. The second is the retable of *Saint Clara* by Luis Borrassà, at the episcopal museum in Vich. How difficult it is for us to give this work a place of its own in our memory !

BARCELONA. THE BARRIO GOTICO.

Among all the paintings glistening with gold and bright colours, we should like to hold the memory of very many of them intact so as to be able to keep up an uninterrupted dialogue with them. The museum at Vich retraces the complete evolution of Catalan painting and, with that of Barcelona, houses the most wondrous collection. The Christs, the Romanesque almost hieratic Virgins — St. Martin, realistic, stern and even tragic in the supremely Christian act of sharing his cloak, bring us up to the admirable retable ;

BARCELONA.
SANTA MARIA
DEL MAR SEEN
FROM
MIRALLERS.

we are particularly impressed by one of its details : the shipwrecked men whom St. Dominic is succouring are clasping their heads like imploring waves. In 1415 this was one of the finest works of the Catalan school.

In the nearby cathedral, José-Maria Sert had done a series of paintings which disappeared when the building was burnt down during the civil war. The sanctuary has been restored and the artist has decorated it with hallucinatory visions done in golden ochre tints. The calvary presents itself in the form of a pyramidal composition of crosses and tortured bodies ; Christ is slipping down into the tomb along an interminable flight of steps ; his executioners are cutting slices of flesh from the body of St. Bartholomew, hanging on his cross.

Above its graceful archways, the cloister with its lofty Gothic arcades is outlined against a splendid patch of sky.

The size of the suburbs, the closely woven network of communications, the excellent nature of the site (a coastal plain between hills) herald the existence of a great city. And Barcelona is indeed more than a great city. Was it not from 874 to 1162 the capital of the independent county of Catalonia ? Did it not defend its privileges against Philip IV by forming an alliance with France and against Philip V by giving itself up to his rival the Archduke ?

Its inhabitants number well over a million. It is the most thickly populated urban centre in the country, its industrial region is the main one in Spain, its port one of the busiest on the Mediterranean. It is a metropolis that knows its own strength and reminds us of the originality of Catalan civilization but it is also a huge city facing resolutely seawards, accessible to progress and constantly increasing.

In the centre and the new nineteenth — and twentieth — century avenues we can stroll wonderstruck by the bustle of the thoroughfares, the number of cafés and the luxuriously dressed shop windows. From the Plaza de Cataluna we go down to the port. Chinatown (the *barrio chino*) offers us the mystery of its narrow, sordid streets, famous for their dance-halls. The wharfs — always slightly nostalgic — afford the imposing and chaotic sight of docks, piers, white liners and dirty tramps. Nothing has a more limited horizon than a busy port when we must view it from a wharf ! But we can overlook it by taking the aerial ferry to Miramar and we shall gaze upon the marvellous panorama of the town and the sea.

Without the wide boulevards, without the gardens, the *ensanche* would be very monotonous : in its streets meeting at right angles the only irregularities are caused by the Diagonal, an interminable thoroughfare which intersects the others obliquely. The modern city has another charm due to the genius of Gaudi the architect. Though their beauty may not at all come up to our taste and standards, many house-fronts, Güell Park and, above all, the Church of the Sagrada Familia, testify to an undeniable power. Notably, many details of the church seem to be lacking in elementary elegance, but this unfinished building — one almost has the impression that it has hardly been begun — already gives an extraordinary idea of an upward surge. And after all we prefer an excess of talent to the monotony of richly decorated monumental imitations which have furnished the inspiration for so many other buildings...

The true interest of Barcelona resides in the group of medieval buildings long encircled by the ramparts. The presence of this group which is not far from the port had been heralded by the small sanctuary called San Pablo del Campo in Catalan ; is it not the oldest Romanesque church in the city ? But its very name indicates that it used to stand in the open country ; the buildings dating from the Catalan Middle Ages await us east of the *ramblas*.

The Ayuntamiento or town hall and the Palace of Parliament open on to the same square ; in the former we shall admire the façade giving on to a side street, with its charming flamboyant windows near which an Archangel Gabriel with wide-spread wings is smiling under a canopy ; the *salon de las cronicas* has been decorated by José-Maria Sert. In 1418, Father Johan decorated the side of the second building which gives on the Calle del Obispo with a St. George, strong and noble in a flowery frame ; this visit affords an incomparable stroll back into the heart of the fifteenth century. Above their slender colonnettes the aristocratically graceful arches of the patio stand out against the sky ; St. George's chapel with its stone lacework increases the delight we take in this edifice built by the master Marc Safont. And we take away with us the memory of the deep courtyard of the Patio de los Naranjos where the gracefulness of late Gothic architecture blends with the first fumbling manifestations of the Renaissance.

One should arrive at St. Eulalia's Cathedral after strolling patiently through the neighbourhood and not go directly to the principal façade which was finished in the nineteenth century and has too much space around it. One should daydream for a short time in the Plaza del Rey edged by the buildings of the old Royal Palace : the great vaulted hall of the Tinell, St. Agueda's chapel, the Records Office of the Crown of Aragon with its severe, noble lines. One should walk along the cathedral walls, stop in front of St. Ivo's door, walk around the apse and along the Calle de la Piedad and Calle del Obispo which encompass the cloister, observe the portals and finally enter the church. Each Spanish cathedral — with a very few exceptions — is a world in itself which never fails to amaze one ; it seems as if all the pictures, the gold plate, the sculpture, the liturgical ornaments live their own separate lives and that a golden dust issues from their beauty or at least from their picturesqueness... To-day little is left of the Romanesque edifice : the present church is Gothic and was built in the fourteenth and fifteenth centuries. It was finished at a later date. The low-reliefs in the *trascoro* represent scenes from the life of St. Eulalia in the sixteenth century. The *coro* has a sumptuous *silleria* dating from the

BARCELONA. THE CLOISTER OF SAN PABLO DEL CAMPO. (XIIITH CENTURY.)

fourteenth and fifteenth centuries. But the altar curtain surmounted by the royal crown which lords it over King Martin's seat is the pride of the cathedral which has nevertheless a rich collection of paintings and sculpture of the Catalan school. In this room, almost entirely of gold, Gothic decoration lavishes its graceful gables. In the cloister, finished in the fifteenth century,

BARCELONA. THE BISHOP'S PALACE.

we might linger long before its many chapels listening to the music of the water playing in the Fountain of the Geese. With its dark, almost black stones, this cool spot suddenly restores all its poetry to the cathedral.

Two of the most beautiful Gothic churches in Barcelona, Santa Maria del Pino and Santa Maria del Mar, were burnt down during the Civil War. Restored to divine worship, they still bear traces of the tragedy from which the whole country suffered.

The Museum of Ancient Art is sumptuously housed in the former Exhibition Palace built in 1929, in front of Montjuich Park, near the Spanish Village. This twelfth-century Virgin of the Annunciation is from "San Pere de Soppe" ; lofty and hieratic, she is spinning busily when the Angel's message reaches her. Romanesque, too, are the struggle between David and Goliath from Santa Maria de Taüll, with its primitive, powerful expression and the extraordinary vision of the Pantocrator from St Clement's, so pathetically and sublimely sincere... But how can we make a choice among the many frescoes that attract our attention ? We shall also remember the sculpture and especially the tense heart-rending lines of the Descent from the Cross from Taüll, or the crucified bodies hanging stiff and bloody on the gallows thus forming a second cross on the instrument of torture...

After the more tranquil thirteenth century, we find once again the great artists whose work we have already admired in the museum at Vich. What a symphony of highly coloured scenes beneath the gilt arcading of the huge retables ! Borrassà shows us the Saviour sitting in state between the episodes of His Passion and His Resurrection ; Ramon de Mur the charming Virgin suckling the Christ Child amidst singing angels ; pensively turned towards a pink-clad Christ Child, the blue and gold Virgin of St. Clara's of Tortosa dreams on between two columns of angels. Finally we feel the Flemish influence which became apparent in the fifteenth century, if only in the folds and the arrangement of the figures in the *Virgin of the Councillors* by Luis Dalmau.

We imagine what these sanctuaries must have been like when adorned with the masterpieces composed for their walls, and what the Catalonia of the Middle Ages must have been like, too, with the vigour of its politics, architecture, painting and sculpture.

To us who are on the first stage of our journey, the Spanish village shows the most picturesque elements of such and such a province reconstituted in a huge *pueblo* : Plaza Mayor de Sangüesa in Navarre, Plaza de Peñaflor of Andalusian inspiration ; another street gives us a foretaste of the revelation we shall have in the Levant. Such a visit is amusing but does not give us a desire to linger. We want to get to know the soul of each province, its irreplaceable atmosphere and landscape, and this village only offers us artificial settings.

Barcelona is never so beautiful as when seen from the heights that rise above it ; some of them may be reached by cable railways. Such is

Mt. Tibidabo which is reached by walking up the Paseo de Gracia; in an intimate Montmartre-like setting, it affords us a sweeping view.

The excursions, both short and long, that may be made from Barcelona are one of its leading attractions. Pedralbes, San Cugat del Vallès and Tarrassà offer us their old churches; Manrèse the memory of St. Ignatius's retreat, and Montserrat the pilgrimage of the Virgin. The monastery is so famous that we hardly dare admit how deceived we are by its buildings most of which have been rebuilt. The true beauty of the spot resides in the surrounding countryside with its jagged horizon — hence the name Montserrat — in the walks to the chapels on the heights, San Miguel's, Santa Cecilia's and San Jeronimo's.

The true garden of Barcelona is in the middle of the sea. We must take the boat some evening and awaken next morning in the bay of Palma de Majorca. The coastline slips by and the port seems to be commanded by the Gothic cathedral, so mighty above the ramparts, and by Mt. Lonja... On Soller Island whose houses follow the perfect circle of a cove, we shall see Miramar where we can closely examine the calm of the deep — a true underwater paradise — and Formentor, the proud headland, inconsolable because it dips eternally into a smiling sea. At Valldemosa stands the flower-scented Carthusian monastery and the dwellings of George Sand and Chopin have been reconstructed; while perfect, almost too perfect — we might say — folk dances await us a few yards away. If possible we shall go as far as the little island of Ibiza lying farther to the south; in the dewy morning light its white houses and geraniums shimmer above the amazed waters.

* **

South of Barcelona the road continues close to the shore and after the summer resort of Sitges, we drive on towards Tarragona.

Washed by the heedless waters of the Mediterranean, it has a rather nostalgically mysterious aspect with the accumulated ruins of several centuries, the memories of Rome and the future Augustus and the old district around the cathedral. The Romans used the gigantic enceinte to erect the imposing fortifications now dominated by the statue of Augustus that rises amidst the ruins in an almost total silence; it is during this walk that we shall come to realize how poetical ruins can be and not when we visit the amphitheatre or Augustus' house defaced by time. The cathedral contains examples of each style that flourished in the peninsula, from the Romanesque to the Churrigueresque. But the unity of style matters little and we long for an unforeseen emotion. At the top of a huge flight of steps, the Gothic portal of the principal façade awaits us and we are perhaps more delighted with the partly Romanesque and partly Gothic cloister with its refreshing music of birds and fountains than with the cathedral

BARCELONA. CHURCH OF THE SAGRADA FAMILIA, BY GAUDI.

itself : how many Spanish cloisters add the attraction of nature to the delicate tracery of stone !

We might drive on along the coast road towards Tortosa and the Levant. But this route goes through a region rather lacking in artistic

MONTSERRAT.

interest before reaching Valencia. Instead let us go to Lerida, stopping at the two Cistercian abbeys founded by Ramon Berenguer IV, Count of Barcelona, in 1157 and 1153 respectively, Santa Creus and Santa Maria of Poblet.

The wide-spread spiritual influence of the monks and their temporal power, the reciprocal help that princes and abbots granted each other — all that is called to mind by our visit to the two monasteries. The sovereigns always found the monks ready to give them help and advice ; they had palaces where they might sojourn not far from the conventual buildings, and a burial place for their eternal rest awaited them in the church. In the Middle Ages the abbeys enjoyed long centuries of prosperity, then came stagnation and decline. During the disorders which upset liberal Spain, the monks were obliged to flee in 1835 and the monasteries were sacked. Now partly restored they diffuse the soothing influence of their semi-ruins over the countryside.

With its lordly alabaster tombs, its two cloisters, and the remains of the palace, Santa Creus must be visited before Poblet ; it must prepare us for it, otherwise the incomparable impression left by the other might handicap it.

Standing at a certain distance from the village, the buildings of Santa Maria of Poblet, dominated by towers and steeples, stretch out in the heart of a smiling countryside, facing a skyline of mountains. We feel a sensation of joy until we reach the first precinct which we enter by the Prades gate. Now we are overwhelmed by a silence of an unusual quality. It is the peace of a partly inhabited monastery, the romantic calm of the ruinous out-buildings which lie on either side of us plunged into an almost human melancholy and the muffled noise from the work in the fields.

We leave the flamboyant chapel of San Jorge with its vault opening out into a star on our right and we go through the Puerta Dorada. In 1564, on the occasion of Philip II's visit, its bronze panels were gilded ; centuries went by, the leaves disappeared, but recently the benefactors of the monastery have presented it with another golden door. At the far end of the Plaza Mayor, just opposite us, stretch the monastery buildings : the Abbot's New Palace, the Torre del Zapatero (the Cobbler's Tower), the church with a baroque façade overlaying the original building, and between two towers the Puerta Real by which we enter.

How many calm and noble visions have succeeded one another beneath the tranquil arches. In the great cloister, the coolness of the central garden and the music from the ornamental pool sheltered by the little temple invade the galleries, one of which is Romanesque and the others Gothic. In the *capilla mayor*, the retable by Damian Forment (1529) superimposes its alabaster tiers where shell-shaped niches abound among the pilasters ; many of them no longer have their statues, alas ; and it has taken great patience to restore the work. In the same way, the recumbent effigies

PALMA DE MAJORCA THE CATHEDRAL SEEN FROM LA LONJA.

of the kings, on both sides of the *altar mayor*, restored by Federico Marès, are once again simple and beautiful, but perhaps exaggeratedly stylized. Then there are the rooms where the monastic existence slipped by amidst

MAJORCA. THE COAST NEAR BANALBUFAR.

AT IBIZA.

the silent peace of the stone walls; the refectory, kitchen, library, the chapter-house, the dormitory for novices and the one doubltess used by lay brothers.

Inside the enclosure there are some quite exquisite buildings — for

TARRAGONA. THE CLOISTER OF THE CATHEDRAL.

instance the *casas nuevas* whose façade reveals on its summit a series of archways like a charming smile on a stern face.

But it will be sufficient to carry away with us the sight of the monastery in front of St. Bernard's pool : a great mass of towers whose reflections cover the glaucous water with shimmering dreams, beneath a pale blue sky, in the balmy air, so spiritual and joyous that it seems almost tender.

Lerida, to which the Great Condé laid an ill-starred siege, will not detain us long. The modern neo-classical cathedral is being restored. The old one, begun in the Romanesque style and carried on in the Gothic period, is still beautiful thanks to the sculpture on its portals and tall tower, but it stands on the hill-top, near the castle occupied by the army and is difficult to reach ; but the splendid view at least rewards one for the climb. After visiting the old districts with their narrow streets, we shall stop at San Lorenzo's Church with its beautiful fourteenth-century retable, then leaving Catalonia we shall enter Aragon.

The most direct road would take us to Saragossa. But making a wide circuit to the north we shall first go to Huesca, formerly the capital of Aragon, which still has its former royal palace and the Gothic cathedral adorned with the very fine retable of the Passion by Damian Forment. Then after stopping at the monastery of Sigena where we find a remarkable chapter-house and royal tombs, we drive on down towards the city of the Virgin of the Pilar.

It appears, powerful and densely populated, among a few trees on the south bank of the Ebro. After the forlorn wastelands frequented by shepherds driving their flocks over the sparse grass of the slopes, it looms up behind the screen of foliage that flourishes near the river. It is very moving at first sight and offers the traveller its two gems : the cathedrals. Its history, too, is moving : since Velazquez sketched the famous view preserved at the Prado, the city has changed considerably — but it still has the same luminous and heroic aspect of a city which, after being the capital of Aragon in the Middle Ages, was obliged to struggle to defend its privileges against Philip II. In 1809 it was to rise up against Marshal Lannes's troops ; during the frightful siege each house became a miniature fortress and the French troops were obliged to reduce them one by one.

What an endless variety of aspects the 'Seo' or ancient cathedral offers us ! Built on the site of a mosque in the Romanesque style of the twelfth century, carried on in the Gothic or Mozarabic of the thirteenth to sixteenth centuries, endowed with an admirable *cimborio* with picturesque tiled roofs, it baffles us continually. In the apse we find here a Romanesque arcade, there a Gothic window, and Moresque elements round about. The façade is baroque as well as the disconcerting tower that goes with

THE MONASTERY OF SANTA CREUS.

THE CLOISTER OF SANTA MARIA DE POBLET (XIIITH CENTURY).

it. Inside, our astonishment will increase. The plan of the almost square church with its five naves reminds us of the mosque it replaced. The delicate feathered Gothic vaults with their capitals adorned with figures and foliage open out into ceiling-roses at their crowns. The retable of the *altar mayor* by Father Johan with its flamboyant canopies pointed like towers, devoted to the life of Christ, the stalls and the walnut lectern which was a gift from Benedict XIII, date from the fifteenth century. The sixteenth century not only left us the *cimborio*, that luminous architectural opening, but also the *trascoro* whose sumptuous decoration is at times a little overdone. The collection of relics and ornaments contains some very fine head-reliquaries and the adjoining museum some admirable medieval Flemish tapestries.

We shall take a stroll around the Seo in its old district full of narrow streets, then we go by the Lonja, where the Gothic mingles with the silver-smith's style, and we reach the Cathedral of the Pilar or New Cathedral.

In January in the year 40 the Virgin appeared to St. James to encourage him in the Apostolate of Spain. On the site of the vision the apostle erected a chapel. In the twelfth century, after the Reconquest, another sanctuary was built, doubtless Romanesque in style ; the spandrel adorned with rosettes and interlacings on Pilar Square may be a vestige of this building. In 1434 the church was burnt down and restored. In 1515 Archbishop Hernando of Aragon had another church, Santa Maria la Mayor, built ; the only traces of the latter are the retable of the *altar mayor* with its statue-laden canopies and pointed gables — the contract for it was signed by Damian Forment in 1509 — the *silleria* and the organ-chest.

Up to that time the history of the edifice was merely that of building and rebuilding, common to so many buildings. But the worship of the miraculous image of the Pilar — the pillar of the apparition on which the statue is placed — had increased to such a degree that Santa Maria la Mayor was raised to the rank of a cathedral in 1675, the equal of the Seo. In 1677, an imposing plan conceived by Herrera el Mozo was worked out in honour of this new title ; the work was begun and carried on in the eighteenth century.

Immense rather than truly majestic — doubtless due to a certain monotony — the building abounds in splendid vaults and cupolas and the setting it offers the Virgin is certainly the most impressive one that the baroque period could imagine. On the one hand, in the cathedral itself with its vaults decorated by Bayeu and Goya, a few elements from the ancient Santa Maria la Mayor have been set in place again ; on the other hand, in a special chapel which is but a receptacle for the miraculous sanctuary, as at the Santa Casa of Loret, the Virgin is worshipped — the statue probably dates from the fourteenth century and is clad in sumptuous robes ; a meditative, moving crowd unceasingly files past in this high place of Spanish piety. The collection of relics and ornaments abounds

LERIDA. A NIGHT VIEW.

SARAGOSSA. THE EBRO AND NUESTRA SENORA DEL PILAR.

in the many gifts that princes and kings have given to Our Lady of the
Pilar.

All over Saragossa we shall look for the traces of its sumptuous past which are somewhat lost in the modern streets of the great city. The Aljaferia is the ancient eleventh-century palace of the Moslem sovereigns; the Catholic Kings enlarged and transformed it. In the ancient Church of Santa Engracia, rebuilt at the end of the nineteenth century, we shall admire the *plateresco* portal where Ferdinand and Isabella are worshipping the Virgin.

In the midst of a wild fascinating countryside south-east of Aragon, Teruel was a city famous for its artistic treasures. During the Civil War, in the winter of 1937-1938, a desperate battle was fought there and the historic buildings were badly damaged. They are not yet completely restored.

Now we go to Old Castile to discover the heart and soul of Spain.

MAJORCA. THE CARTHUSIAN MONASTERY AT VALLDEMOSA.

NEAR BURGOS. THE MONASTERY OF LAS HUELGAS.

LANDSCAPE BETWEEN SEVILLE AND AVILA.

CHAPTER II

OLD CASTILE

CASTILE alone reveals the national soul. One word, it seems, suffices to describe this region : it is the land of the

BURGOS MUSEUM.
ENAMELLED RETABLE FROM SILOS.

73

spiritual. In the likeness of the luminous souls of St. Theresa and St. John of the Cross, it is the barrenness of the earth beneath the Creator's dazzling eyes.

The very dust of the cities breathes forth glory, that of the countryside is golden with sunbeams; at night the deep blue sky where innumerable stars twinkle is wonderful. The cathedrals and even the humble churches abound in retables, sculptures and collections of relics and ornaments; there are countless castles and palaces.

But the lesson to be drawn is quite different. It is that of the permanency of the atmosphere and soul. Neither the sky nor the inhabitants' expression have changed since the days of its greatness. Castilians still have the noble bearing and speak the clear-cut language of kings.

It is not only a question of permanency but also of diversity. The aridity of the tablelands is not uniform. There is abundant foliage in the north, so little water is necessary to create fertility... Castile and its inhabitants are divided between austerity and barrenness on the one hand, and cool, smiling landscapes on the other.

Soria affords us our first sight of this country : a Romanesque town with a reddish patina, on a mountainous site. Before crossing the bridge that spans the Duero, we enter the ruins of San Juan's monastery. Beside the church, the Mozarabic cloister intertwines its arches in mid-air; the upward surge of the arcades whose vaults have disappeared, resembles a very graceful cavalcade in the intense light. Once across the river, we discover the collegiate church of San Pedro, dating from the twelfth to sixteenth centuries; around the central garden extend the galleries of its cloister, supported by double columns. The palace of the Counts of Gomara offers us a beautiful Renaissance façade, and Santo Domingo's church a Romanesque portal whose figures overburden the curves of the arches and radiate around the spandrel. In the Museo Numantino are kept the relics of ancient Numantia whose site lies a few miles to the north.

If we had to discover, for some of the great cities of Spain, the tonality in which the colours of the sky and stone blend, the appropriate key-note of Burgos would be silvery grey — a soft, precious ash grey, both gay and proud, — which wraps the towers of its cathedral in a poetic light. The city epitomizes the art and struggles of Gothic Castile, but, in their turn, its spires symbolize the city : " Two sharp, jagged spires ", wrote Théophile Gautier, "stamped out, festooned and embroidered, with the smallest details chiselled out like the setting of a ring ; they soar heavenwards with all the fervour of religious faith and all the transport of an unshakable conviction..." Then in the centre of the transept one's eye dwells upon the open-work lantern-tower adorned with pinnacles which is less visible and even more extraordinary and, beyond it, on the High Constable's Chapel.

BURGOS CATHEDRAL. THE CRUCERO.

BURGOS CATHEDRAL.

Under the profusion of the upper parts dating from the fifteenth and sixteenth centuries, are the foundations dating from the thirteenth. The first stone of this edifice was laid in 1221 or 1222 by Bishop Maurice; the model chosen was Bourges Cathedral, or those of Le Mans and Coutances which are derived from it. In the middle of the century, the work was

PILLAR IN THE AMBULATORY. THE CIRCUMCISION.

directed by the master mason Henry who also worked in Leon. The sculptures on the portal also drew their inspiration from France, the models being the main façades of Notre Dame in Paris and Notre Dame in Rheims. Only those on the transept doors remain : the Puerta del Sarmental on the south side, the Puerta Alta (the street is above the level of the floor of the sanctuary) on the

THE ESCALERA
DORADA.

BURGOS. THE NAVE OF THE CATHEDRAL.

BURGO

VIEW.

BURGOS. THE CASA DE MIRANDA : THE PATIO.

THE CARTHUSIAN MONASTERY OF MIRAFLORES.
DETAIL OF THE RETABLE OF THE HIGH ALTAR.

north side. Afterwards, according to the usual custom in Spanish churches, each period embellished the cathedral with a new structure; for instance,

PALENCIA. SAN MIGUEL CHURCH.

the fourteenth century left us the cloister. In the fifteenth and sixteenth centuries the chief additions were due to three architects of German origin : John, Francis and Simon of Cologne. Among other architectural or decorative works, John was the creator of the spires ; Simon, of the chapel of the High Constable of Castile, Don Pedro Hernandez de Velasco ;¦Francis, of the Puerta de la Pellejeria and, assisted by Juan de Vallejo, of the admirable lantern.

We must approach the cathedral as we would the most precious of treasures and watch for the apparition of its various aspects at the end of streets which modify the perspective. For the moment, let us take the Calle de la Paloma, follow the cloister walls, admire the Puerta del Sarmental and gaze upon the main façade, paying particular attention to the upward surge of the towers rather than to the portals whose statues were removed in the eighteenth century. We climb up on to the terrace of St. Nicholas's church and walk up the Calle de Fernan Gonzalez. There we are several yards above the cathedral whose beauty is everchanging ; then we go back down to the Puerta de la Pellejeria whose graceful sculpture evokes the free and flourishing Renaissance, still untouched by austerity, and its arcade leads us into the edifice. But let us rather imagine we are going in through the Puerta Alta ; Diego de Siloé's *Escalera dorada* with its double bannisters is a regal descent and a few steps farther on we find ourselves beneath the *cimborio ;* the flood of light from this basket-work of ethereal architecture lights up the tombstones of the Cid and Jimena.

Théophile Gautier's lines are still the most beautiful that have ever been written about this marvellous cathedral : "It is such an abyss of sculpture, arabesques, statues, colonnettes, ribs, lancet-arches, pendentives that it makes one giddy. Even if one looked at it for two whole years, one would not have seen everything. It is as compact as a cabbage, as fenestrated as a fish-slice ; it is as gigantic as a pyramid and as delicate as a woman's ear-ring, and it is impossible to understand how such filigree can have maintained itself in the air for so many centuries !"

After the lantern, we visit the Constable's chapel in the centre of the apse : the retable (on which a Frenchman, Philip Vigarny, worked), the tombs, the decoration and iron railings would be worthy of a second cathedral. We shall discover some admirable sculpture on the tombs or in the cloister (for instance, the smiling and majestic Doña Violante de Aragon), paintings, and *objets d'art* which would constitute one of the richest museums imaginable — the recumbent effigy of Bishop Maurice, one of the finest of the "works of Limoges". We shall find picturesque relics, such as the chest the Cid filled with sand and iron to deceive the Jewish money-lenders ; we shall see the amusing *Papamoscas*, that is to say the human fly-catcher — when he rings the hour, he opens his mouth as if to swallow these insects. Not far from there is worshipped the famous

VALLADOLID. THE FAÇADE OF SAN PABLO'S CHURCH.

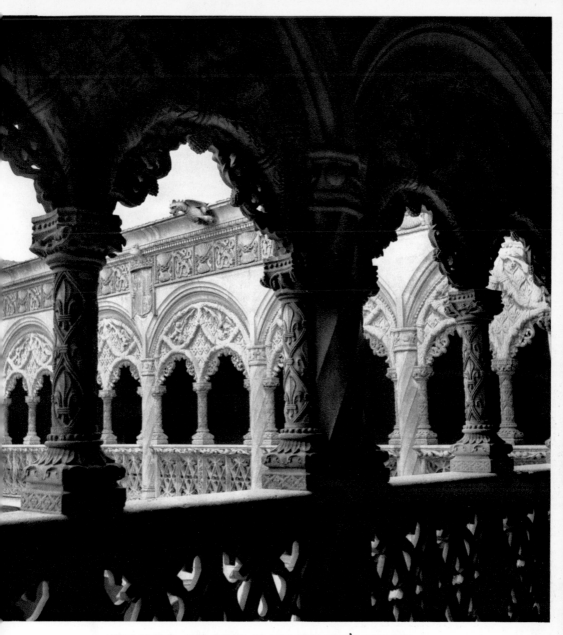

VALLADOLID. THE PATIO OF SAN GREGORIO'S COLLEGE.

Christ made of skin, with long hair and eyebrows; its exaggerated tragic art satisfies the Spanish taste for the ghastly.

As for the retables and architectural beauty of the cathedral, we shall find them again in the Gothic churches of the city. The *altar mayor* of

85

San Nicolas is worth a visit in itself; San Esteban, whose main façade opens on to the countryside, brings us back to the heart of nature; San Gil is the most majestic one of all. Civil architecture in the Casa del Cordon and the Casa del Condestable offers us an indefinable something which is both proud and resolute; in the Arco de Santa Maria (a gate erected in honour of Charles V on the site of an ancient tower) there is an indefinable breadth and solidity; for Burgos was a martial city which has kept part of its walls and erected a monument in memory of the hero born within them on the site of the Cid's house. The spirit of the city consists of a memorable grandeur and also of a smiling attitude towards life : the Plaza Mayor, dominated by the statue of Charles III, and the Paseo del Espolon are animated, and bordered by pleasant-looking shop-windows. After visiting the historic buildings we must make a pilgrimage to the provincial museum housed in the Arco de Santa Maria and admire above all one of the first funerary monuments in Spain, by Gil de Siloé : it is the tomb of Juan de Padilla, Isabella the Catholic's page, killed at the capture of Granada; even the work in the museums takes us back to the Reconquest, heroism and death. Then we shall stroll through the modern city; is it not possible for the *cafeterias* and shops of today to reflect the different soul of each city ?

It is hardly necessary to go out of Burgos to visit Las Huelgas Abbey, founded in 1175 by Alfonso VIII : the cloister is Romanesque, the church and monastic buildings Gothic, but the royal resting-places and the fabrics found in the tombs are far more interesting. The final impression is not free from austerity and contrast with the ornamental display of the retable and tombs of the Carthusian monastery of Miraflores, also near the city; Gil de Siloé and Diego de la Cruz made the retable; Gil de Siloé alone did the tombs of King John II, his wife and the Infante Alonso (very similar to Juan de Padilla's). Around the kneeling prince, the foliage and angels coil in graceful motifs; the sovereigns' effigies lie on a polygonal base adorned with innumerable statuettes; this art is simply exquisite, and seldom does an artist reach this degree without ceasing to move us.

Unfortunately the Abbey of Silos is almost forty miles from Burgos; it was restored during the last century by French Benedictines but the Romanesque cloister with its extraordinary capitals and moving sculpture shows medieval art at its greatest and thus brings to a happy end our artistic tour of this region.

How pleasant it is to discover cities like Palencia : unexpected and little known, less famous than its great neighbours and yet so arresting because of its animation and originality. A street bordered with arcades crosses it from end to end following a delightful curve. The Calle Mayor is so attractive that it is difficult to imagine that there can be inhabited houses beyond it as well as interesting churches like San Pablo. However,

86

the cathedral looms up at a bend in the street ; it is a powerful mass that both disconcerts and intrigues us for it has no façade and not even a well-preserved porch — but inside it abounds in treasures : Flemish tapestries, goldsmiths' work, retables, *silleria*, paintings.

The road takes us on to Valladolid, monotonous and uninteresting. The city which was the capital where Philip III re-established the seat of his government for some years, has kept the proud aspect of its past : churches hidden in narrow streets, a Royal Palace considerably altered, a cathedral whose plans were drawn by Herrera, the architect of the Escurial, and which has remained unfinished, Cervantes' house and the beautiful façade of the Colegio de Santa Cruz.

The unforgettable is to be found elsewhere.

Let us cross the big grey mercantile city. Suddenly we discover the arcades of the Plaza Mayor and those of the Fuente Dorada square. We are in front of San Pablo's church. Built in the days of the Catholic Kings, its powerful and monumental façade was composed like an erudite poem.

A few yards behind stands the Colegio San Gregorio, of approximately the same period. Its imposing porch and its patio have poetry as well as skill : two strange barbarians mount guard at the door, the columns of the arcades rise between open balustrades and the upper parts of the galleries are adorned with stone lacework of an almost luminous quality. The finest museum of polychrome sculpture in Spain has been installed in the edifice and presented in the most modern way : as we go from room to room we find examples of pre-eminently national and popular art. The retable of San Benito el Real (brought from a nearby monastery) by the painter and sculptor Alonso Berruguete, indicates not so much the influence of Michel-angelo as an original interpretation of spiritual anguish through bodily torture : can we ever forget St. Sebastian, whom the last arrow failed to kill ? Isaac not yet saved by the Angel's hand ? The exaggeration of Juan de Juni, though he was of French descent, and of Gregorio Fernandez amazes us even more, yet their very violence is part of their genius.

The *pasos* remind us of Good Friday here ; the solemn, contemplative ceremonies are among the finest in Spain. Castilian soberness would not adapt itself to the Andalusian atmosphere and it is the tragic aspect of the Passion that the procession of holy statues evokes in this city.

We shall find this majestic gravity throughout the province. The castles recall the battles of yore, even if their destiny has changed — Simancas houses the Spanish Records Office : even if ruin has overtaken them — like Medina del Campo. The very smallest towns, if they could make glorious history relive in their noble dwellings and sanctuaries, would have a tale to tell the traveller ; and they can always offer him artistic treasures — for instance, Medina de Rio Seco, a dusty village with un-forgettable retables. At Tordesillas, in the ancient Mozarabic palace, now the monastery of Santa Clara, the enchanting decoration tragically

87

AVILA. THE GATE OF THE CARMELITES.

AVILA. THE CITY SEEN FROM THE CONVENT OF THE INCARNATION.

evokes Joanna the Madwoman who only died in 1555 after living through almost the entire reign of her son Charles V.

From Valladolid to Avila the road climbs to an altitude of 3400 feet, the mountains become bleak, the ranges block the horizon with their black or grey masses, the chaotic heaps of huge boulders become more numerous ;

only the olive trees add a gay touch to the austerity of the landscape. It is impossible to define the spiritual presence that can be felt in the very air we breathe : the dimension of the sierras, the barrenness of the countryside covered only with boulders or sparse, scanty crops, the clearness of the sky with its merciless light ; all is rough, plain and serene. Avila appears — and the sight is unforgettable. Moreover it is the impression of Castile that the traveller from France after a night in the train gets when he awakes ; up to now he has seen only a wilderness, and suddenly he catches sight of a flock of towers encircling an old city, of the outer districts tumbling down from the surrounding walls as if they were the skirts of its stone garment ; the train stops for a few minutes and sets off again, but the stirring memory of the city remains engraved in our minds with all the small details left by a first impression.

We take great care not to enter Avila immediately. First we stroll along the foot of the ramparts among the little churches of the suburbs — some are delightful and delectable. We shall stop at the convent of the Encarnacion which was that of St. Theresa. It has a humble aspect and looks like a big farm whose inhabitants lead a happy life without troubling themselves too much about the agitation in the outside world ; the parlour where the saint used to converse with St. Peter of Alcantara has remained untouched ; a little glass cabinet contains some relics, and we are moved to see a humble ceramic pot of which copies are still made in the region ; thus the traditions of craftsmanship enable us to rediscover a little of the daily life in a sixteenth-century convent.

We walk slowly towards the distant city. Its solemn silence draws us like a mystery. It is not only cold because it is built on the summits but also because it can endure only an austere landscape around it.

We cross the Rio Adaja and stop at a kind of temple lightly set on a small mound : *las cuatro postes* — the four columns. Avila will perhaps win our hearts even more when seen from here. Elsewhere in the world there are a certain number of fortified towns. Without mentioning the size of its enceinte, the peculiar quality of this one is the fact that one can take it in at one glance. It spreads over the slopes and the mountain top. At first the eye singles out the lower line of ramparts, then the city, finally the upper part of the fortifications dominated by the cathedral ; it is a chain of poems in stone, scanned by the innumerable towers in the harsh light, while the Sierra de Gredos looms up westwards, mighty and dark. But the oratory of the *cuatro postes* is not only a view point or a graceful oratory ; it recalls an episode in St. Theresa's life. When very young, she ran away from her father's house with her brother ; she was found on this spot and taken back to the city. In no other place — with the exception of the convent of the Encarnacion — shall we feel her presence to such a degree as here; we see the city, on the very edge of the barren countryside symbolizing spiritual adventure.

How could we find the sublime austerity of this soul in the baroque church, raised within the walls on the site of her birth-place ?

Let us enter Avila by way of the Rastro Gate. The noise of the town, hardly rising above the silence, muffles the noises of the world. We immediately come upon a typical inn, dazzling white and adorned with flowers ; then as we wander among the austere, massive *casas solariegas*, we reach the cathedral. The façade was altered in the eighteenth century, but the clear-cut, lofty aspect of the building, most of which was built in the twelfth century in the days of Master Fruchel and in the thirteenth and fourteenth centuries, was hardly affected. The transept still has a portal adorned with Gothic sculpture and the apse, projecting into the enceinte, is part of the defensive system. Inside, it is mighty, sober and confined though the Renaissance lavished graceful decoration upon it : in the *trascoro*, the pillars on both sides of the *capilla mayor*, and the tomb of Bishop Fernandez de Madrigal whose serious face is quite untouched by the sumptuous decoration around it. Pedro Berruguete worked on the retable of the *altar mayor*.

The architecture of the cathedral bears witness to close contact with France and also with St. James-of-Compostella. San Vicente's church might be compared to edifices in Burgundy and the south of France. Begun in the Romanesque style and continued in the Gothic, its main façade has a sculptured portal which may be the finest one in Spain after that of Santiago. Inside, on the tomb of St. Vincent and his sisters, the agony of the martyrs is depicted with pathetic simplicity.

At a certain distance from there, below the ramparts, the Dominican convent of Santo Tomas is famous for its memories of the Catholic Kings and Torquemada. The sovereigns' son, Prince John, is buried there in the Italianate tomb by Domenico Fancelli. But we admire above all the life of St. Thomas told by Pedro Berruguete and we are moved by the serenity of the nearby countryside with its barren Castilian landscape.

Let us wander through the streets at random ; the women wear long black veils and full skirts belted at the waist, sometimes with big floral motifs near the hem. We shall see even more of these costumes in the surrounding *pueblos* than in the city. But what a quantity of things we shall find in the latter ! Fabrics, whitish ceramics with little blue flowers, donkey-blankets, with parallel multicoloured stripes and straw hats as huge as monstrous flowers — Avila keeps all these things in store for us in its shops and network of alleys.

It is above all the spiritual aspect of the city that cannot be discovered in a single day. We must see it at nightfall and at the break of day when it is so cool that we almost shiver as we walk down the slopes of the outskirts. We meet old black-clad women and milk-sellers urging their phlegmatic donkeys along. We are forever discovering another palace or an unknown building — the Casa de Polentinos in the *plateresco* style or the Capilla de Mosén Rubin, as pure as a Greek cross treated in the Renaissance fashion...

AVILA CATHEDRAL. THE MONUMENT OF BISHOP FERNANDEZ DE MADRIGAL,
CALLED EL TOSTADO, BY VASCO DE LA ZARZA (DETAIL).

It is only once we are as serene as Avila that we can leave it — with the hope of breathing the air of the summits once again.

Segovia, rather like Toledo to which it may be compared for the beauty of its site, its magnificent historic buildings and its delightful atmosphere, is built on a rocky spur surrounded by the Eresma and Clamores rivers ; above their junction towers the tapering mass of the Alcazar, perched on steep cliffs. We must walk round the city till we reach a pine-clad hill to the south to gaze upon it. At dusk, the sky is an extraordinary lavender blue ; opposite us the cathedral looks like a ship scudding along, giving the impression of rising and plunging into the air and the latter retreats progressively into a bluish transparency ; the medieval churches on our right loom up amidst the houses ; in the background the Roman aqueduct raises its haughty architecture. The scene has an almost Florentine sweetness and harmony.

Harmony is perhaps the most suitable word for Segovia. Its inhabitants smile, its streets swarm with life. We are in an open city which reveals itself to us quite quickly, at least on the surface.

From our pine-clad hill, we walk down the Cuesta de los Hoyos and reach the aqueduct, stopping to look at the curious Romanesque churches with outside galleries. On the square of the Roman Azoquejo[1] we find ourselves at the foot of the famous arches over which the water for the city continues to flow. We shall appreciate the graceful majesty of the series of arcades even more if we climb up to a certain height on the left ; the landscape stretches behind the timeless galleries ; its serenity and austere charm were here long before they came into existence and yet they seem to represent the cavalcade of eternity itself.

Turning our backs on the countryside, we go up the street leading to the Casa de los Picos whose façade is adorned with diamond-shaped stones, and to the little square in front of St. Martin's church ; the nearby palaces enhance the latter's charm as well as its porch adorned with tall statues and the columns of its Romanesque gallery. Near the Plaza Mayor, the transept of the cathedral stands out against the sky. The immense mass of the edifice stretches out, harmonious and graceful ; the golden gleams of the sun play on the warm tonality of its walls. Juan Gil de Hontañon and his son built it in the sixteenth century but the cloister dates back to the fifteenth century. Among the works preserved in the cathedral, the most famous one is perhaps, the excessively dramatic *Descent from the Cross* by Juan de Juni.

In the picturesque, hilly by-streets, there is a profusion of emblazoned house fronts. San Esteban and its tower, and the severe and well-balanced bishop's palace, form one of the most evocative groups in Segovia.

(1) Aqueduct.

Just outside the city, Parral Monastery, dating from the fifteenth and sixteenth centuries, and the chapel of the Vera Cruz, built by the Templars with a polygonal layout, invite us to continue our walk into the nearby country. Beyond the chapel, we soon find a village of low-

SEGOVIA. IN THE SHADOW OF THE AQUEDUCT.

SEGOVIA. THE ALCAZAR.

roofed houses, along whose streets stroll peasant women in the eternal black garments — and thus one of the traveller's fondest wishes comes true : to get to know the countryside unknown to tourists.

A few miles from Segovia, at San Ildefonso de la Granja, stands the palace built bv Philip V in memory of his French childhood. The palace,

SEGOVIA. THE CATHEDRAL SEEN FROM THE SLOPE OF LOS HOYOS.

whose façade on to the park is Italianized, is especially interesting because
a few of the tapestries of the former royal collection are shown there —

THE PALACE OF LA GRANJA : THE PATIO DE LA HERRADURA.

SIMANCAS. ENTRANCE TO THE CASTLE.

it is still one of the most marvellous. What we discover in the gardens is
not an imitation of Versailles but a transposition. The style is that of the

early eighteenth century and aims rather at gracefulness than majesty; the irreplaceable beauty of the flower-beds comes neither from their layout nor their greenery but from the abundance of water supplied by the neighbouring sierra. Is it not a sweet emotion for a Frenchman to travel through the heart of the mountains of Castile and discover there a memory of Versailles — not an insipid adaptation but an original work with delicate shades in the statues and trees ?

Segovia and La Granja are the joyful smile of their province. The Carthusian monastery of Parral or the memory of St. John of the Cross in his native Arevalo are its mystical aspect. Castles, like that of Coca which is a group of innumerable towers, re-tell its warlike past.

And the whole of Old Castile is also austerity and freshness and a hymn from the soul.

VALLADOLID MUSEUM.
ST. SEBASTIAN BY BERRUGUETE.

MADRID. THE FOUNTAIN OF NEPTUNE.

MADRID. THE GRAN VIA AND THE FOUNTAIN OF CIBELES.

CHAPTER III

NEW CASTILE

MADRID, long considered a poor relation of the great European capitals with their more magnificent historic buildings, is as complex as a woman, as noisy as a stroll through a perpetual fair, and charming withal because of its animation. It contains different towns either juxtaposed or mingled ; that of the Hapsburgs, the eighteenth-century town with the wide

MADRID. THE FAÇADE OF THE ROYAL PALACE.

MADRID. RETIRO PARK.

promenade so popular in the century of light, that of the end of the nineteenth century and the beginning of the twentieth with its geometrical quarters and great housing blocks, copies of all sorts of styles ; American thoroughfares with monumental sky-scrapers and bronze groups hovering on the roofs. What a long distance it has had to cover before becoming this gay, attractive city with its countless noises !

Reconquered by Alfonso VI at the end of the eleventh century, it was one of the bulwarks of the struggle against the Moors, but in those days there was no hint of its prodigious destiny. It was but a little town where the Cortès sometimes met and whose Alcazar was frequented by royalty. Ferdinand and Isabella used to stay at the Convent of San Jeronimo el Real (the church, dating from that period, was badly restored during the nineteenth century). Charles the Fifth of Germany kept Francis I of France a prisoner in the Alcazar after the battle of Pavia and began to transform the fortress into a palace. During his reign the noble family of Vargas arranged the chapel whose retable and tombs (above all that of Gutierre, Bishop of Plasencia, hence the familiar name of "Capilla del Obispo", the Bishop's chapel) constitute one of the finest architectural groups that can still be seen in the city.

In 1561 Philip II decided to establish his residence in Madrid for reasons which still remain obscure — but among which the desire to give united Spain a new capital, quite independent of the old ones like Burgos and Toledo and situated in the geographical centre of the peninsula, must certainly have been the dominating factor. But its growth was artificial. The king was chiefly engrossed by the Escurial. The palace-monastery was the artistic and political centre of the Spanish State. The sovereign merely transformed the Alcazar and built Segovia Bridge, a splendid work over a paltry river, the Manzanarès, jeered at for its scarcity of water.

Under Philip III, despite the fact that the court was temporarily transferred to Valladolid, and under Philip IV a few public buildings worthy of a capital were built. A style was born, faithful to Herrera's manner, that counteracted the invasion of the baroque ; it reminds one of the plain, noble Escurial, and makes lavish use of the picturesque bell-turrets of which Philipp II had been so fond in Flanders ; we even find them at San Lorenzo[1]. The Plaza Mayor dates from this period ; it was built between 1617 and 1619, was burned down several times and rebuilt. Great festivals were held there as well as *autos-da-fé* and executions ; adorned with the equestrian statues of Philip III by Jean Bologne and Tacca, it still preserves the memory of the public life of the last Hapsburgs and their Madrilenian subjects, in a rather dirty popular district smelling of fish. Not far from there, the Carcel de Corte (i. e. the noble prison, now

(1) San Lorenzo del Escurial, the palace-monastery of the Escurial whose architect was Herrera.

MADRID. TOLEDO BRIDGE.

the Ministry of Foreign Affairs) and the Ayuntamiento, altered since that time, are fine examples of the style of the palaces of the period. The most important one, that of Buen-Retiro, has disappeared ; it was terribly damaged by the French and English during the War of Independence, only a few scattered buildings remain — the Museum of Artistic Reproductions, the Army Museum with the Hall of Kingdoms, formerly the most beautiful one in the castle, adorned with Velazquez' *Spears*, royal portraits by this painter, battle scenes, and Zurbaran's series of the *Labours of Hercules* — an admirable collection housed in the Prado ; the gardens of the Retiro perpetuate the memory of the former park, but the monumental style of the nineteenth century colonnade erected in memory of Alfonso XII has driven away evocations of the seventeenth century.

Under Philip V, Pedro de Ribera represented Madrilenian baroque in buildings whose lavish decoration cannot hide the general nobility of line. After the church of the Virgen del Puerto, finished in 1718, he built San Fernando's Hospice (1722-1726), now the Municipal Museum, with its amazing gates whose ornamental waves never tire of unwinding their curves, and Toledo Bridge (1719-1731), so majestic and flowery, so over-burdened with oratories and fountains.

But with the first Bourbon and Elizabeth Farnèse came the influence of France and Italy. The Alcazar having burnt down on Christmas Eve, 1734, the building of a new palace was entrusted to the Italians, Juvara and Sacchetti. Neither Philip V nor Ferdinand VI lived to see the work finished ; it was only Charles III who settled in the Palacio de Oriente for the first time in 1769. The Convent of the Salesas Reales was built by a Frenchman, François Carlier, the son of one of the creators of La Granja ; Queen Barbara of Braganza who had the buildings erected, was buried there with her husband.

The true creator of this spacious Madrid, adorned with promenades and buildings in the antique style, was Charles III. Raised in memory of his triumphal entry into the city, the graceful mass of the Puerta de Alcala was Sabatini's work. Ventura Rodriguez laid out the promenade of the Prado, decorated with the very popular fountain of Cibeles (Cybela) drawn by two lions, and those of Neptune, Apollo and the Seasons. Villanueva was the architect of the Prado, which was originally built to house natural history collections, and of the porch of the nearby Botanical Gardens.

Under Charles IV, when Maria-Louisa and Godoy dominated the court, life in Madrid knew a charm which Goya rendered most delightfully in his tapestries and in certain parts of the decoration of San Antonio de la Florida. But the French invasion put an end to this happy time ; the days of the Dos (second) and Tres (third) de Mayo 1808 gave the signal for the War of Independence.

During most of the nineteenth century, Madrid, a liberal city, had its share of the political uncertainty of the period. Once calm was re-established at the end of the century, the city grew in size and wealth ; new residential sections were created. The movement continued until the events of 1936 with the creation of the Gran Via. Since then, the gigantic buildings of the new ministries and the sky-scraper on the Plaza de España bear witness to the capital's desire to grow like an American boom town. And its composite style based on imitations has finally given birth to a manner of its own which is at once youthful, excessive and amusing. It would be impossible to imagine a more perfect setting for the animation of the Madrid of today.

How bustling and charming life in this capital is ! Beneath the arches of the Puerta de Alcala we can contemplate the long thoroughfare of the same name ; it is cut in two places by Cibeles and the junction of the Gran Via. We go by the Post Office — scoffers have dubbed it : Our Lady of the Postal Services — and the War Office, Godoy's former residence. Then we catch sight of some inordinately high buildings. Their conception generally reminds us somewhat of the Monterrey Palace in Salamanca, and somewhat of the Escurial with a few columns and a bronze group flying uncomfortably skyward topping the whole. The baroque façades of the churches of Las Calatravas and San José nestle between their modern neighbours. This juxtaposition will accompany us as far as the Puerta del Sol.

This square, which takes its name from the Gate of the Sun — it no longer exists — is the heart of the capital. Semi-circular and bordered by indifferent buildings — the most beautiful of them is the one built by the Frenchman, Marquet, under Charles III — it has taken on a daintily provincial air since fountains were installed there in the middle of the lawns. The lack of majesty is fully compensated by the incessant traffic, the abundance of cafés and shops and the picturesque aspect of the crowd. Calm and collected policemen direct pedestrian traffic according to the colour of the traffic lights and the shrill sound of electric bells. In the evening the people of Madrid run for taxis which are too few and far between ; the queues grow longer and longer at the bus stops ; hawkers offer cigarettes ; beggars, sometimes horribly mutilated, beg for a *parrita* — alms ; the blind sell lottery tickets, uttering a guttural shriek that would pierce the most implacable night : *sale hoy* — 'Drawing today', and the *limpiabotas*, pointing at dirty shoes with a significant gesture, energetically invite the passer-by to have them polished.

It is on the Gran Via that the crowd in Madrid seems most dense. The sky-scraper of the Telefonica rises there and around it the jabbering crowd hardly seems to move. Along a thoroughfare interrupted by two medium-sized squares, those of the Callao and the Red de San Luis, open the most sumptuous shops and beautiful *cafeterias* : he who has not drunk a coffee *con leche* or eaten *gambas* (prawns) or a *tortita à la plancha* (a kind of pancake), in one of the latter, cannot call himself a true Madrilenian !

And of course the sight afforded by the Plaza Monumental during a bullfight is even more motley. In front of the bullring in the Moresque

MADRID. THE GRAN VIA.

style, ticket-sellers, people selling fans and paper sun-hats accost you, offering their different wares. Everything changes — when the fight finally begins in the ring. After the solemn parade of *alguazils* on horseback,

MADRID. MARKET NEAR THE RASTRO.

MADRID. THE PRADO : DETAIL FROM TITIAN'S CHARLES V AT MUHLBERG.

THE PRADO. VELAZQUEZ : DETAIL FROM THE MAIDENS OF NOBLE RANK.
DONA ISABEL DE VELASCO.

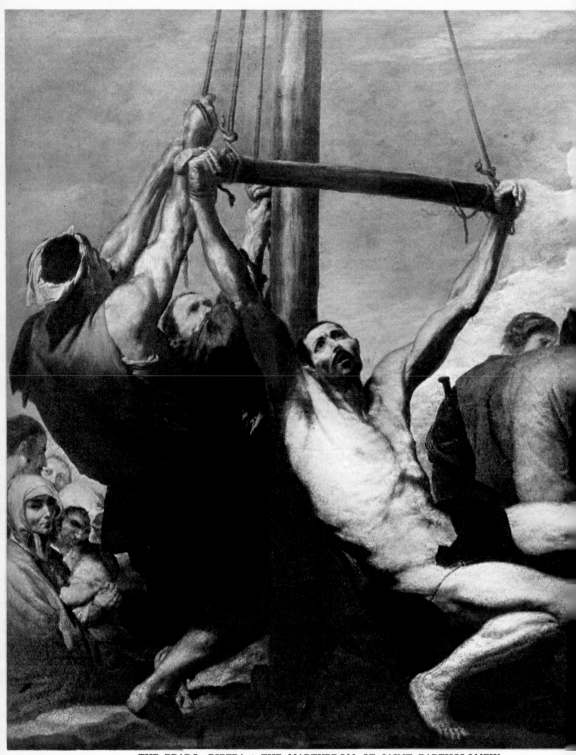

THE PRADO. RIBERA : THE MARTYRDOM OF SAINT BARTHOLOMEW.

GOYA. DON FRANSISCO DE PAULA ANTONIO.

picadors, banderilleros, toreros, the scene of putting the bull to death often unfolds like a heroic ballet in which death constantly hovers around the man before satisfying itself with the animal. Picadors on horseback are the first to thrust their points into the beast. The latter, already weakened by the blood it is losing, grows weaker still when *banderilleros* place *banderillas* with an elegant and daring gesture. Finally, the *matador,* alone in the ring, puts the bull to death after different passes. On the tiers, the crowd, half of it in the shade, the other half in the sun, waves fans whose variegated hues are dimmed or inflamed by the light ; everybody shrieks in answer to the *torero's* gesture and this *ole* ! bears witness to the common excitement of thousands of spectators.

Such is Madrid the picturesque. But the capital is more than that. If, like Toledo or Salamanca, the city is not a museum in itself, it is truly the city of museums.

To bear comparison with these two marvellous cities, it would need more atmosphere and its treasures, though abundant, would still be insufficient : the old districts of the Plaza Mayor, San Francisco el Grande, San Isidro, Goya's paintings at San Antonio de la Florida and his *Communion of St. Joseph of Calasanz* at San Anton, and finally Lope de Vega's house. But how many of its museums are too seldom visited ! The Royal Palace is admirably situated opposite the sierra whose colours are the very ones painted by Velazquez ; towards the centre of the city it stretches along the Plaza de Oriente adorned with the fine equestrian statue of Philip IV by Tacca ; it houses a small room whose walls are sheathed with Retiro porcelain, part of the Royal Collection of tapestries, and a collection of arms which is perhaps the finest one in the world — and on the ceiling of the Throne Room, Tiepolo painted the peoples of the Spanish monarchy in a very successful and picturesque symphony. The Lazaro Galdiano museum and that of the Royal Academy of San Fernando, to mention only two, are among the most interesting that can be seen in any city ; the former because of the motley whole formed by its collections, the latter for its very beautiful *Monks* by Zurbaran, the *Burial of the Sardine* and several portraits by Goya.

But Madrid is above all the city of the Prado.

It was one dynasty — the Hapsburgs — who, as they reigned over most of Europe, and especially over Italy and Flanders, were in a position to know the most famous artists and acquire their works easily by placing orders with them. Philip IV, a mediocre politician, was a patron of the arts and Velazquez's friend — what sovereign has ever had such a portrait-painter continually at his heels ? It was another dynasty — the Bourbons — who were deprived of many of the treasures of past reigns by the unfortunate burning of the Alcazar but who were able to recognize Goya's genius and later to found the Prado. To this foundation of royal origin, gifts and purchases have been added and today the museum is one of the most homogeneous and the most varied in the world. Homogeneous thanks to its Spanish paintings ; varied because of its pictures representative of Continental schools (England alone is ill provided for) and its paintings by Titian, Veronese, Tintoretto, Rubens...

The fact that the Prado is irreplaceable reveals itself little by little with works such as the *Spears* — or the *Menines*[1] — the perfection of painting thrown into the shade by the perfection of life itself — or *Charles IV's Family*. To their individual presence so many canvases by Velazquez or Goya are added that the complete evolution of the artist can be followed — then comes the place occupied by each of them, and those who emulated their glory, El Greco, Ribera, Zurbaran, Murillo, in the whole history of Spanish art — and finally the comparison between this art and that of foreign schools brings out its originality which is the passionate attraction of a realism with numberless accents. Spiritual truth in El Greco reduces the bodies to flames of flesh. The artist in Velazquez seems to be supremely unmoved. The tortures of St. Bartholomew by Ribera do not prevent the painter from bathing in a grave mysticism his *Repentant Magdalen* or *Jacob* plunged in his divine dream. Murillo's reality is not always that of hearts easily moved to pity and Zurbaran's reality, issuing from a monk's believing soul, suffuses his canvases with an unforgettable light.

If, on leaving the Prado, one were obliged to linger before a picture — before a single one — Titian's *Charles Vth of Germany at Mühlberg* would arrest our attention for a long time. The helmeted, armed prince, galloping along on his steed, as he aims his lance, is a sublime incarnation by this Italian genius. He rises above himself, he is *the Emperor and Victory* — but on his furrowed features, among the grey tints of the canvas, blows a mortal wind and to our minds wandering through the domain of poetry it seems that there is an invisible companion at his side : this companion is Dürer's *Knight* about to be seized by *Death;* are not they both of them heroes of the epic march of humanity advancing — in spite of its victories — towards the universal end of things ?

The meaning of this epic — and that of the Catholic faith that explains it — are intimately blended in the blood of the Hapsburgs and the soul of the Spanish race. Charles V was to retire to Yuste ; Philip II to build the Escurial. But the homage was the same : it was rendered to the Master of life and death.

⋆[⋆]⋆

The barrenness of the landscape prepares us for the severe majesty of San Lorenzo. The mountains rise in three tones : first little rolling tablelands whose golden or russet tints are dotted with scattered shrubs ; farther on, a zone of low hills, almost black from being scorched by the

(1) Maidens of noble rank attached as companions to princesses of the blood.

THE ESCURIAL. NORTH FAÇADE.

GUADALAJARA. THE PALACE OF THE DUKES OF THE INFANTADO.

sun; finally the Sierra de Guadarrama which ostentatiously displays its peaks as if it wanted to stretch as far as possible along the horizon. And the monastery appears grey like the mountains and the atmosphere ; a wonderful stair-head set by man on the side of a Sinaï that might be the dwelling of a redoubtable God.

It would be purely arbitrary to compare the Escurial to Versailles. Their only common point would be their immensity on the one hand, and on the other the general unity of creations emerging from the brain of a unique being. The former is a convent and a royal pantheon. Charged by Charles V to erect a burial-place, for him, Philip II fulfilled this duty by commemorating the victory of St. Quentin, gained on St. Laurence's day in 1557, and by repairing a ruined convent in the city. Nothing proves that the king ever thought of imitating the appearance of the rack on which the martyr was tortured ; a more simple explanation of the layout might be that it was inspired by St. John the Baptist's Hospital in Toledo.

The Escurial is the convent where Spain, face to face with its defunct kings, glorifies its Catholic mission in prayer. Versailles is the palace of the monarchical idea expressed by the myth of Apollo.

The first stone of San Lorenzo was laid by Philip II on April 23, 1563. The work, supervised by Juan Bautista de Toledo and Juan de Herrera as well as by the sovereign in person, lasted twenty-five years ; the founder was able to enjoy the work of art he had conceived and carried out. The edifice is a blending of the Spanish tradition, memories of antiquity and the Italian Renaissance, and of certain elements of Flemish origin. Just imagine the daily sight of oxen dragging the stones, quarried in the sierra and even hewn on the spot, up the mountainside ! Just imagine the impressive arrival of the royal coffins : those of Isabella of Valois, Don Carlos, Charles V, his wife and sisters !

We walk around the buildings whose natural austerity is softened by corner turrets and storeys of varying heights, and enter the main courtyard — the Patio de los Reyes ; it takes its name from the monumental statues of the Kings of Judea adorning the church front. The inside of the latter is luminous, graceful and sober and impresses us by its resemblance to St. Peter's in Rome. On both sides, in the *capilla mayor*, and the pillared galleries — the work of Pompeo Leoni — stand rows of royal groups in a magnificent kneeling posture : Charles V, the Empress Isabella, the Emperor's sisters on the north side ; Philip II, Don Carlos, three of the king's four wives (Mary Tudor is not represented), on the south side.

Just below the sanctuary is the Royal Pantheon, laid out by Philip III and Philip IV. All the kings of Spain since Charles V and the dowager queens lie there[1]. Before reaching this supreme retreat, the bodies had

(1) With the exception of : Philip V and Isabella Farnèse, buried at La Granja, Ferdinand VI and Barbara of Braganza at the Salesas Reales in Madrid. On the other hand, Isabella of Bourbon, Philip IV's first wife and Henry IV's daughter, lies in the Royal Pantheon as her husband desired although their son Baltasar Carlos died before coming to the throne.

to remain for ten years in an adjoining room, whose mere name — the *pudridero* — evokes the attraction of the Spanish soul to the macabre and everlasting nothingness amidst so much religious ostentation and hope — and this purifying halt represents for the sovereigns the tribute offered to Christian humility before attaining the royal immortality of the Pantheon.

The next rooms, filled with the tombs of *infantes*, *infantas* and queens, date from the nineteenth century : their ugliness and pretentiousness are distressing. There lie Don Juan of Austria who was victorious at Lepanto, and Vendôme, Henry IV's grandson and a soldier of genius, who died in Spain just after saving Philip V's throne ; the youthful king rewarded him by giving him a place among the princes.

How many treasures we must ignore : objects of art or paintings ! If only we might linger in the admirable cloisters like that of the Evangelists ! Among the pictures in the sacristy we find the last great work of the School of Madrid, the swan-song of the Hapsburg court ; by a skilful effect of perspective Claudio Coello represented Charles II and his train worshipping the *Sagrada Forma* or miraculous Host that Rudolph II gave Philip II, in the sacristy itself. In the chapter-house we go from marvel to marvel. El Greco is the first to attract us to this spot where he failed to please. Here is the *Dream of Philip II*, a crown of glory where God lets the king enter ; here is the *St. Maurice* which the king refused to place on the high altar : he had ordered a scene of martyrdom and the painter offered him this heroic deliberation of youthful soldiers already radiant with eternity. Velazquez is represented by an episode from the story of Joseph : the brothers displaying the blood-stained tunic before their father. What attentive and mystical gravity we find in Ribera's *Jacob tending Laban's flock* ! *Outraged Christ* by Bosch shows the circle of odious heads encompassing the Unforgettable Face. The *Crucifixion* by R. van der Weyden is at once tragic and awe-inspiring ; the Lord under torture, His Mother, John the Apostle, alone in a sculptural arrangement — the splendour of red and grey. The *Descent from the Cross* by the same artist is an old copy of the original picture in the Prado yet it does not fail to move us.

The plainness of Philip II's rooms — he died there in 1598 after an atrocious week's journey in a sedan-chair from Madrid to the monastery — contrast with those of Charles III and Charles IV, which are light and gay, decorated in the Pompeian style or hung with tapestries by Goya and Bayeu. Their atmosphere is also found in the Casita del Principe that Charles III had built for his son by Villanueva who was to be rendered illustrious by the Prado : in the small drawing-rooms there is an abundance of gilt-enlivened white furniture, Retiro ceramics and precious objects.

At some distance from the monastery, Philip II's *silla* is the stone seat where the king used to supervise the work : in front of us, the silver grey mass of the Escurial, dominated by its cupola, stands out against the dark mountains. But our last vision is almost smiling — that of the

SIGUENZA. THE PLAZA MAYOR AND THE CATHEDRAL.

SIGUENZA CATHEDRAL. THE TOMB OF THE DONCEL IN SAN JUAN'S CHAPEL.

south side of the convent, of the Gallery of the Convalescents and the Friars' Garden : the reflections of the buildings floating on the pool in the silence of the air and the calm of the water.

Near Madrid, the Pardo, a Hapsburg castle which was considerably enlarged in the eighteenth century, has become the residence of the Head of the State. East of the capital the Civil War caused enormous damage to Alcala de Henares and Guadalajara ; the former city, which owed part of its splendour to Ximenez's buildings, has not been completely restored ; the second one, famous for the *plateresco* palace of the dukes of the Infantado, now has only a mutilated façade and patio left. In the same direction, but much farther away on the borders of New Castile, Siguenza awaits us ; it is so picturesque with its castle, the arcades of its Plaza Mayor and its streets lined with emblazoned houses. The cathedral, whose severely powerful façade is brightened up by a very simple rose-window, juxtaposes the Romanesque, Gothic and *plateresco* styles in a pleasant harmony, and contains the tomb — some say it is the finest one in Spain — of Doncel Martin Vazquez de Arce killed in 1486 before Granada : the youth, leaning on his elbows, reading an open book, seems already to possess eternity.

Art seldom moves us by such very simple means.

To the south, Aranjuez, a former royal residence, is less notable for its castle — there is nothing very remarkable except a porcelain closet similar to the one in the Royal Palace in Madrid ; the other rooms offer nothing of major importance — than for its gardens along the Tagus, where the princely barges still shown to visitors used to sail. At some distance from there, the Casa del Labrador, a sort of Little Trianon, like that of the Escurial, displays its succession of exquisitely charming Pompeian drawing-rooms and their lifeless charm fills the visitor with an unutterable melancholy.

But Toledo, the city so wondrous for its atmosphere, its Mozarabic buildings, its memories of El Greco and its cathedral, lures us on towards its secrets. On the way from Madrid, a few pictures by the great artist seen at Illescas have prepared us for the city which he really adopted as his own : now we are gazing upon it and we demand of it an enchantment more magnificent than our most beautiful dreams.

On our left, on the heights, stands the fourteenth-century San Servando castle and the new buildings of the Military Academy, which was housed in the Alcazar before the Civil War. On the right, in a loop of the Tagus, between sheer bluffs, Toledo appears, preceded by Alcantara Bridge dominated by its cathedral and bearing the wound of a ruined spot — that of the Alcazar and its surroundings.

Many civilizations have accumulated on the site of the city : Rome, the Visigoths, the Arabs, the Kings of Castile, Ferdinand and Isabella, and Charles V have left their marks on the town. Nature had not only supplied the setting — the almost circular gorge of the river — but also the sign, the symbol of the city : the dazzling shower of sunbeams which lights up the landscape and the very air we breathe with an indefinable spiritual fire. Toledo a dead city ? Yes, if "dead" can be applied to a city where for many a long year the inhabitants have been content to keep in repair the buildings dating from its glorious past and to lead a vegetative, limited life. But Toledo has another very animated existence; if dust could speak here, it would express itself in the language of the spirit for it comes from the stone hewn for churches and admirable historic buildings.

Let us not cross Alcantara Bridge, built in the thirteenth century by Alfonso X and slightly modified by the Catholic Kings and Philip II; let us take the road on the other bank of the Tagus which encircles the city from afar. Whatever the time of day may be, it seems as if Toledo were on fire; an inner fire that consumes it and only lets us see its radiance and phosphorescence; the steeples, towers and cupolas vibrate in the indescribable reflections spread by a hidden conflagration; the cathedral becomes a silver ship against the sky. The glare of the sun and the diffused radiance of the city blend into a blaze of light which would be recognizable as that of Toledo among a thousand other "High Places alive with the same presence."

Even the noise made by fire is not lacking. The voice of the city is the muted din of a crowd murmuring a difficult, age-old poem to itself, its music the rustling of a forest ready to emigrate to another planet and sending the signal for departure from bough to bough. The counterpoint is the shrill cry of cicadas scattered through the hill amidst the estates to which they have given their names : the *cigarrales*.

We enter the city by way of the San Martin Bridge, also built by Alfonso X and restored by Archbishop Pedro Tenorio — we know what great prestige and what an enormous influence the archbishops of Toledo, the Primates of Spain, enjoyed. In the very first buildings we see, we realize the truth of Barrès's sentence : "The argument of Toledo is a superb dialogue between Christian and Arab culture which assail each other and then mingle." Would not that be an excellent though obviously literary definition of Mozarabic art ?

On the rising ground near the San Martin Bridge stands the nave of San Juan de los Reyes the outside of which is decorated with the chains of the Christian captives that Ferdinand rescued at Malaga and Almeria. The church abounds in memories of the Catholic Kings — *los Reyes*. To commemorate the victory of Toro, they founded the monastery and entrusted it to the Franciscans whose first novice was the future Ximenez; their resting-places were to be put in the chapel. But the capture of Granada changed their plans and the edifice, begun in 1476 by Juan Guas and carried on by Enrique de Egas, rose very slowly. Part of the outbuildings were ruined by the French occupation. Today there remain the cloister and the church which bear witness to the delightful new elegance of really Spanish Gothic architecture in the days of the Catholic Kings. Isabella's style, *plateresco* style, whatever its name may be, it blends "the forms and processes of Gothic art, Italian art and Arab art."[1]

(1) Elie Lambert — *Tolede* — The best work one can read on art in Toledo.

THE RAMPARTS OF TOLEDO.

TOLEDO. THE CHANCEL OF THE CATHEDRAL.

TOLEDO CATHEDRAL. THE VIRGIN OF THE CHANCEL.

Nearby, the most representative examples of Mozarabic art await us. Santa Maria la Blanca, the old synagogue, offers us a trite façade in an almost wild garden; but inside, the naves constitute a high-ceilinged room whose white columns support capitals adorned with scrolls, pinecones and strap work; filigree work runs along the walls above the arches. It shows what a great influence Andalusian art had in Toledo in the thirteenth

century although we cannot determine its date exactly. We must
date the neighbouring synagogue of the Transito from the following

TOLEDO. SANTA MARIA LA BLANCA.

TOLEDO. SAN JUAN DE LOS REYES. THE APSE.

TOLEDO. THE STREET OF THE BITTER WELL.

TOLEDO. THE GARDEN OF LA CASA DEL GRECO.

century — it takes its name from the chapel consecrated to the death — or *transito* — of the Virgin, subsequently established within its walls. As majestic and delicate as the hall of a palace, it shows us the elements of a decoration that we shall find once again in a more exiguous setting, at the Taller del Moro or at the Casa de Mesa.

Who does not know the view of Toledo in which El Greco expressed

TOLEDO. SANTO TOME. EL GRECO : THE BURIAL OF THE COUNT OF ORGAZ (DETAIL).

the identity of his soul with the city ? This picture seems to sum up the history of this artist of Cretan origin, who was Titian's pupil ; after his *St. Maurice* failed to please Philip II, he settled in Toledo and became the inspired interpreter of Spanish society in his day — as a foreigner he may have understood the depths of its character better. At the same time he painted religious pictures for the countless convents and churches of the city. We can discern an evolution in his work. The first Toledan paintings are the retable of Santo Domingo el Antiguo, ordered in 1577 (the *Assumption*, in the centre, has been replaced by a copy), the *Espolio* of the cathedral (where we see his tormentors stripping Christ of his tunic) in 1579 and *The Burial of the Count of Orgaz* (1586). The *Assumption* in the museum of San Vicente's church is an example of his work at the end of his life, with even more evanescent forms and indefinable colours — a spiritual world where clouds, landscapes and beings become torches before the eyes of God.

The Casa del Greco is the reconstitution of a Toledan home like the one where the painter may have lived ; in the rooms opening on to a patio full of greenery, there is period furniture, and in a little building nearby a number of his works have been brought together. At some distance from there, in the old church of Santo Tomé, with its Mozarabic tower, we find *The Burial of the Count of Orgaz* at the back of a chapel. The lower part shows the entombment of the count by St. Augustine and St. Stephen who, according to the legend, were supposed to have come to do this moving homage to the dead man : the scene is a series of admirable portraits in a severely religious setting ; the upper part, of an entirely different inspiration, shows the splendour of Heaven, mingling clouds and angels' wings in inexpressible forms.

We walk along picturesque by-streets to reach the cathedral and, after going by the archbishop's palace which is joined to it by an arch-shaped bridge, we come out on to the square : opposite us stands the town hall on which El Greco's son worked ; on the left rises the main façade of the cathedral with its portals framed between the lofty tower and the cupola of the Mozarabic chapel. How can a few lines suffice to speak of the sanctuary which probably houses more treasures within its walls, with their complex history, than any other church in the peninsula ? Begun about 1225, on the site of a mosque, it was originally planned as the same type of church as the builders of Notre Dame in Paris, the cathedral of Bourges and the chancel of Mans cathedral were trying to erect. One Petrus Petri worked there in the thirteenth century, but the main work was practically finished only at the end of the fifteenth century, and the upper part of the *capilla mayor* was even rebuilt at the beginning of the sixteenth. In the stone framework which was generally built with an eye to the original plan, subsequent modifications and decorations brought about countless changes. The essential spirit of Toledo cathedral lies

133

in this duality; it abounds in an incredible profusion of retables, iron gates, tombs, sculpture, and paintings in a nave that was to embody a type of cathedral of a style even purer than that of its French models. Just as luxuriant vegetation invades buildings standing in forests, so Toledo has decked the stone vessel that has foundered on its flank with its multiple aspects.

We can only admire in passing the sculpture on the transept doors — the Lions' Door and the Feria Door. What a world of treasures the inside offers our inquiring eyes! Here is the place where the Virgin gave the scapular to St. Ildefonse. Rodrigo Aleman worked on the choir stalls where he depicted episodes from the capture of Granada, and Philip Vigarny and Alonso Berruguete carved the upper seats; in the centre a French Virgin reminds us of the wide-spread influence of French art in the Middle Ages. The huge retable of the high altar retraces scenes from the life of Christ in its tiers of pictures : on either side stand the royal tombs placed above one another; that of Cardinal Mendoza, with its Italianate architecture, surpasses them all in splendour. Sumptuous and imposing Renaissance gates separate the *coro* from the *crucero* — they are the work of Domingo de Cespedes — those of the *capilla mayor* are the work of Villalpando.

How astonished we are in the apse when we discover the *Trasparente* arranged by Narciso Tomé between 1720 and 1732. In the Churrigueresque style, it is an imposing display of marble and bronze, a multiple flight of angels above a Virgin and Child; this decoration frames the hole which lets light in through the vault. Not far away, in St. James's chapel, stand the tombs of Don Alvaro de Luna and his wife, by Pablo Ortiz (1489); they are moving beyond all others. In St. Ildefonse's chapel lies Cardinal Albornoz. And we must still admire, only to mention a few of the treasures of this cathedral, the Moresque ceiling of the ante-chamber of the chapter-house, the ceiling of the latter, John of Burgundy's frescoes and finally the relics and ornaments.

We shall take away with us our vision of El Greco's paintings, not only the *Espolio* but also the *Apostles* distributed over the walls of the sacristy whose vault was decorated with fresco paintings by Lucas Giordan.

And our stroll through Toledo continues. In Zocodover Square, the centre of the city, we mingle with the excited crowd. Then we visit the Alcazar, so often burnt down and rebuilt; it was the scene of the heroic resistance of General Moscardo and his cadets during the Civil War. In the same district, the Santa Cruz Hospital, built by Enrique de Egas during the first half of the sixteenth century, offers us its admirably embellished façade.

How many artistic treasures of the first rank this city still has in store for us. Cardinal Tavera's tomb by Alonso Berruguete at St. John the Baptist's Hospital dates from the Renaissance, but the Puerta del Sol goes back to the fourteenth century and the front of the nearby church of Cristo de la Luz is a tenth-century mosque.

South of the city, the light becomes merciless and floods the monotonous tracts which prolong New Castile towards Andalusia. Manzanarès Castle, whose mighty bulk seems to vie with the mountains, and Ciudad Real, fortified of yore, might symbolize La Mancha — resplendence of the sun, receding solitudes, a void that even the imagination would tire of creating...

Our itinerary leads us south-east of Madrid towards the Levant. Cuenca is encircled by gigantic crags whose very aspect suggests actual ramparts : at the very spot where they become a ridge, tall, straight houses rise into the air where they seem to remain suspended — the *casas colgadas*. It is in and around Cuenca that the stones are magically alive ; about nineteen miles to the north the *ciudad encantada* multiplies the number of rocks with their astonishing shapes...

TOLEDO. A COURTYARD.

ALICANTE. THE PORT AND THE CASTLE OF SANTA BARBARA.

THE RICE-FIELDS OF THE ALBUFERA.

CHAPTER IV

THE LEVANT

Bᴇᴛᴡᴇᴇɴ Catalonia and Andalusia, the coast of the Levant offers us a succession of coastal plains separated by mountainous heads. That is where we find the great cities, ports and fertile *huertas*, that is where we see

137

the play of the varied colours of the crops and houses in the dazzling Mediterranean sunlight. A rich land, a happy land contrasting with the sierras rising behind with their sharply outlined contours and sparse population.

Valencia, with its large population (it is the third city in Spain), its port (second to Barcelona), and wonderfully fertile countryside is one of

VALENCIA. THE CATHEDRAL : CIMBORIO SEEN FROM THE MIGUELETE.

VALENCIA. THE HARBOUR.

ALBUFERA. A FISHERMAN.

the provincial capitals of the peninsula, ranking almost with Seville or the
capital of Catalonia.

The centre of the city is the huge triangular square now bearing the
Caudillo's name. The modern façade of the Ayuntamiento, formerly an
eighteenth-century house, the Post Office, shops and cafés form the rather
trite setting where we may see the essence of life in Valencia. But the
flower-market lends its originality, and the trams, incessantly rattling past,
the crowd trampling by and the hum of the city remind us of the fact

PENISCOLA. FISHING WITH A CAST-NET.

ALICANTE. THE FEAST OF SAINT-JOHN : BURNING THE FALLAS.

that the Spaniard loves to live in the street. Great thoroughfares extend in all directions. We must stroll there for some time to realize how modern Valencia has developed and grown in power — then we must escape from it and go to the ancient city with its thousand and one aspects : the trading city which built one of the most beautiful Lonjas in the medieval world, the city that lavished its art in God's service on its cathedral and the retables in its museum, the proud city defended by its towers — the prosperous baroque city overflowing with imagination. Valencia with its thousand faces, so full of life beneath its flawless sky !

The interesting historic buildings are situated between the Plaza del Caudillo and the Rio Turia. Opposite the modern market we are attracted by the fine flamboyant façade of the Lonja de la Seda or Silk Hall. It bears witness to the power of the middle class in the fifteenth century and does not fail to remind us of the splendours of Flemish cities. Supervised by Father Compte and J. Iborra, work on it lasted from 1483 to 1498. The wing of the Consulado, with its upper gallery laden with Renaissance motifs, was only finished in 1548. How beautiful the tall flamboyant windows are, topped by the sixteenth-century storey. The very plain tower, the gabled portal, between two bays likewise flamboyant, and the battlements crowning the whole, are exceptionally stately and simple. Inside the great hall supports its airy arches with the help of finely ribbed, wreathed columns : the Lonja of Palma which served as a model is surpassed here.

The neighbouring church of San Juan del Mercado has kept its baroque façade but after the devastation of the Civil War, the interior with its frescoes by Palomino and its luxurious decoration only gives us a very poor idea of the splendour of Valencian baroque which is to be found everywhere in its churches and palaces.

After admiring, in a narrow street, the graceful, picturesque tower of Santa Catalina, dating from the fourteenth century but restored later on, we set off for the cathedral. The different styles that have succeeded one another in Spain are represented in the edifice built on the site of a mosque, as was often the case. The Palau door is Romanesque, that of the Apostles is Gothic ; the main walls are Gothic, too, and above all the lantern with its fine silhouette, which sheds light on the nave like incense from heaven. On the Plaza de la Seo, there is a two-storeyed Renaissance gallery ; the main façade is adorned with a baroque portal and near it stands the Miguelete Tower named after its big bell ; it is very popular in Valencia and was built between 1381 and 1429.

The retable of the *altar mayor* is protected by two huge volets whose paintings depict scenes from the life of Christ and the Virgin Mary. In a side-chapel, Goya retraced episodes from the life of St. Francis Borgia. But the marvel of the cathedral is the ancient chapter-house. The ground plan is square, bearing an octagonal vault, and a rich, flamboyant decorative

143

scheme frames the altar of the Santo Caliz, the richly set agate cup supposed to be that of the Holy Grail.

Near the Apostles' door, the chapel of the Virgen de los Desemparados — the Virgin of Waifs and Strays — is a sumptuous baroque composition, and in the same district the Audencia displays its buildings, partly Gothic and partly Renaissance.

The Colegio del Patriarca, a Romanesque palace dating from the end of the sixteenth century, is a true museum. In the private apartments the pictures are presented in the intimate atmosphere we so dearly love to find around certain works of art. Among all those in the Colegio we shall select the *Adoration of the Shepherds* by El Greco, a symphony in grey whose figures seem even more evanescent than stretched out, suspended or carried away into the air ; having recovered hope through the birth of the Saviour, the world ignores the burden and weight of sin.

What a contrast the Marquis de Dos Aguas' palace forms with sixteenth-century architecture ! It seems as though waves have broken over the house and been changed into sculpture by men, still hesitating between the two states. Yet it only affords us an attenuated aspect of its original decoration. Hipolito Rovira Brocandell, the painter — who died mad — had decorated the outside but his work was done away with in the nineteenth century. But in the middle of the Churrigueresque façade, owing to the youthful, merry imagination of Ignacio Vergara, we can still see, in the first storey, the statue of a Virgin and Child in an undulating niche, and below it, on both sides of the main door, the weirdly contorted and draped men that symbolize the waters. A very fine collection of Hispano-Moresque ceramics was installed here recently.

Through picturesque streets — narrow, wayward, thronging with people — we reach the Torres de Serrano. For the traveller who arrives in Valencia from the opposite direction to ours, crossing the bridge of the same name (1518), they afford a majestic entrance amid the ancient buildings and a far-reaching view over the *huerta*, seen from the top of them. They were raised after the model of the Puerta Real de Poblet by Pedro Balaguer between 1392 and 1397. In their turn they served to inspire the architect of the Torres de Cuarte ; the latter, situated in another part of Valencia add memories of the castles of Southern Italy to those that are purely Spanish. Is not the Levant one of the Spanish provinces open to international exchange in trade, art and thought ? Didn't the kings of Aragon rule over Valencia and Naples ?

On the other side of Trinidad Bridge, the oldest one in the city (1402), the provincial museum offers us its collection of Valencian Primitives. The fifteenth-century triptych, the *Virgen de la leche*, shows the Virgin suckling the Christ Child, and on the volets of the retable are small portraits of saints. Doubtless the most beautiful retable is that of the *Puridad*, partly painted by Nicolas Falco and sculptured by Pablo, Onofrio and

ELCHE. THE PALM GROVE.

Damian Forment (1502). The museum also possesses beautiful works by Juan de Flandes, and saints by Francisco Ribalta, from the Carthusian monastery of Porta Coeli. In the picture where Velazquez painted his own face, we recognize his strong features and abundant hair ; Goya is present here with several portraits, especially those of Bayeu and Rafael Esteve Bonet and also that of a delightful group of children playing on a swing. Among the foreign schools we especially notice a *Virgen* by Pinturicchio and a *Christ Insulted* by Bosch.

The festivals in Valencia are above all famous for their flowers. The *Fallas* are tall cardboard and wooden constructions that are borne through the streets and which have become one of the touristic attractions of the city ; they are solemnly burned on St. Joseph's day.

A visit to the capital of the Levant can be completed by excursions to nearby spots. The port of Grao can be reached from the centre of the city by tram. The Lagoon of Albufera, separated from the sea by a narrow spit of land, is edged with rice-fields. Manisès perpetuates the tradition of its ceramics — called Hispano-Moresque — with their metallic reflections. This art came from Malaga and its region and had its hey-day in the fourteenth and fifteenth centuries. The Carthusian monasteries of Porta Coeli and Liria offer us their historic buildings...

Northwards, Sagunto (Saguntum), so silent and proud, seems never to have forgotten the siege it was subjected to, so many centuries ago, by Hannibal. It has the ruins of a Roman theatre and on the heights a castle whose enceinte extends all along the hill. Independent Sagunto, Rome and the Arabs built on the same site ; now there remain only aloes, cacti and wild plants amid the impressive vestiges of the fortifications, facing a sweeping landscape in the calm air which vibrates with the happy flights of birds. Castellon de la Plana is quite lacking in interest and from here on the only thing that attracts us is the steep rock of Peñiscola, overlooking the sea in a picturesque situation : Benedict XIII took refuge in this castle at the ends of the earth ; in the absence of Christianity which was escaping from his authority, nature afforded him one of the most majestic landscapes on the Spanish coast of the Mediterranean and we can imagine the thoughts of this half of God reduced to an eagle's nest amongst the waves.

Southwards, Jativa, crowned by a fortified castle, Gandia and its collegiate church adorned with a retable by Damian Forment, full of memories of the Borgias, Alexander VI, the scandalous pope and Francis the saint, lead us towards Alicante. The Churrigueresque façade of the Ayuntamiento recalls the blooming of baroque art in the Levant. Then Elche takes us into the dreamland of its African palm groves, the only ones in Europe.

Must Murcia be called the languorous city ? Among its white-washed walls, a hint of nonchalance seems to float, doubtless due to the sometimes unbearable heat. *Toldos*, or tents, cover the two main streets, the Plateria

LANDSCAPE BETWEEN VERA AND ALMERIA.

MURCIA CATHEDRAL. THE CHAPEL OF LOS VELEZ.

and the Traperia. Along the Rio Segura stretch gardens where the bright colours of flowers blaze in the shade of palm trees.

The cathedral, begun in 1394,* had been finished in the sixteenth century, but after the floods of the Segura it had to be rebuilt in the eighteenth century. The chapel of Los Velez dating from the end of the fifteenth and beginning of the sixteenth centuries evokes the manueline style of Portugal with its octogonal form ; outside it is decorated with escutcheons and chains, inside with a profusion of lace-work arcades and canopies below an inscription. On the main façade is displayed a baroque decoration

148

of columns, arches and niches ; it is elegant without being massive and animated but not exaggeratedly so. From the tower, almost 300 feet high, the view takes in the *huerta* in a dusty haze of sunlight and foliage.

It was in Murcia that popular sculpture had its last burst of glory — with Salzillo — in the eighteenth century. The museum holds the amazing Crib with its countless figures that he composed, thus giving us a true

MURCIA. THE ERMITA DE JESUS : THE LAST SUPPER, BY SALZILLO.

CARTAGENA. VIEW OF THE NAVAL BASE.

picture of the costumes of his day in the Levant ; but his principal claim
to glory is the sculptured *pasos* that have been preserved at the Ermita
de Jesus : the *Dolorosa* or Our Lady of Sorrows, the *Last Supper*, the *Oracion
del Huerto*, the *Prayer in the Garden*, that is to say, Christ in the Garden
of Olives. Too tearful in appearance, the figures — so different from our
conception of deep feeling — only come to the front in the Holy Week
processions.

Lorca, lying inland, and Cartagena, on the coast, will be our last
memories of the Levant — dazzling colours on the sea, steep mountains
covered with castles, and the moving beauty of gilt retables.

NEAR CARTAGENA. MILL OF LA CERCO.

MARBELLA. LEAVING THE HARBOUR.

GRANADA. THE GARDENS OF THE ALHAMBRA.

CHAPTER V

ANDALUSIA

ON San Fernando's square in Seville, two English girls, lovely and gay as birds in the morning, get into a brand new open vehicle with their father; it is a *jardinera* and an incomparably imposing coachman drives them to the *Feria*; he was waiting near his carriage and immediately

153

answered their call. He lets the travellers admire the festival at leisure and then he drives them to the "Venta di Eritaño" and discreetly gives the order to entertain them royally. Scarcely half an hour later, "made

ALMERIA. ON THE QUAYS.

rather lively by *manzanilla* and completely intoxicated by the air and the sunlight of this Sevillan April", the foreigners ask for their bill; in vain. They are obliged to leave without paying and, in the same carriage, driven by the same coachman, they return to their hotel. Not only the travellers but also the coachman are received with great respect. The latter then explains the reason with the utmost politeness : he happened to be near the *jardinera* and did not want to disappoint the girls when they called him ; and then, without revealing his name, the fascinating coachman disappears like a mysterious prince. The waiter tells his amazed guests that it was a young Sevillan of the highest lineage and as the English express their astonishment at seeing such a great personage consent to pass for a humble coachman, their interlocutor replies : *"No, por eso mismo ; porque es un gran señor"* — "That is precisely why he did it ; because he is a great nobleman."

This anecdote which Manuel Machado tells with a delightful sense of irony and poetry, is an admirable evocation of a certain Andalusian atmosphere, not that of stereotyped literature or folklore but another which is more intimate and subtle, and constitutes the irreplaceable attraction of this region.

We shall admire young couples whose charm is centuries-old: the man, slender, tall, with an almost black skin, plastered hair ; the woman with a slightly dancing gait and lightly curling hair.

Andalusia is the land of songs, dances, feasts, joy and melancholy, ardour and fatalism — an impassioned Christian woman who has not forgotten nearby Africa lying but a few leagues beyond the sea. Holy Weeks and *Ferias*, popular mirth and deep piety, wild mountains and a sun-drenched coast, olive groves and sumptuous villas, fantastically huge cathedrals as in Seville, Arab buildings and gardens — Andalusia, spray of roses and mystery edging the hem of the severe mantle of Castile.

The Coast

Almeria, the first of its great ports, offers itself to us — the brother of Algeciras and Cadiz, but to tell the truth, it is more like Cartagena and Alicante : built on a site that cannot be altered there is always the kinship of the wide tree-planted boulevards and the wonderful blue sky and sea. The white houses still imbued with memories of the Moors, spread out or clustered together between the heights and the port opening on to the gulf.

In this city, so rightly called the mirror of the sea, we feel that everything turns into brightness and gaiety. The resplendent light, the luxuriant vegetation, do not make us forget the historic buildings : the Alcazaba, built by Abd er Rhaman III, from which we have a fine view over the city and sea ; the church of Santiago, built in the Renaissance style and topped by a mighty tower ; last of all the cathedral. On its site rose a mosque which

MALAGA. VIEW OF THE RAMPARTS CONNECTING THE ALCAZABA
WITH THE CASTILLO OF GIBRALFARO.

had become the cathedral after the Reconquest but it was destroyed by an earthquake at the beginning of the sixteenth century. It was rebuilt in the Renaissance style of the school of Granada.

The road from Almeria to Malaga is one of the most beautiful drives that can be taken in the mountains along the sea. We go deep into the heart of the desert heights and only see the Mediterranean again just before reaching the small town of Adra : the port, amidst the sugar-cane, still has the ruins of its castle. Then as far as Motril there are only fishing villages, and stretches along a winding road lying a few yards from the sea which disappears or suddenly re-appears in a splendour of which we never tire ; the dark tint of the mountains fades amidst the varied tones of the cultivated fields and the brilliant sky. Motril stands at a certain distance from the shore on which a small separate port has been set up ; on the site, baked by the sun, stand two churches and countless houses ; but the poverty-stricken lie on the pavements and when the bus goes by — an event in these out-of-the-way towns — the curiosity of the inhabitants is only aroused for a few minutes. It is in such a *pueblo* that we can get to know the eternal life of Andalusia, magnificent and wretched, blighted and glorious ; lavish of the only source of wealth common to all Andalusians : light. In Almuñecar, the boats, as is so often the case in small ports in Spain and Portugal, are merely drawn up on the tawny sand ; the ruins of the castle, the eternal fields of sugar-cane, the leprous houses in the precipitous streets, the coloured clothes hanging from the windows, attract us to the town despite its destitution. Nerja, and Torre del Mar, so many halts on the road which winds up and down so cleverly facing the unchanging blue of the deep.

Malaga has undergone earthquakes and the Civil War. In the cool of the shade and the fountains we drive along the *paseos* bordering the sea or circling the Gibralfaro ; at the end of the flowery avenues we find the inn which the Tourist Administration has opened, facing a panorama of sea and gardens. The Fine Arts Museum houses some interesting works and the cathedral is a splendid Renaissance edifice said to have been planned by Diego de Siloé and Diego Vergara and continued in the eighteenth century ; one of the two towers is unfinished, thus giving the building its peculiar appearance ; inside, the *silleria* in the *coro* contains some very beautiful statues by Pedro de Mena. On Good Friday, the processions here are among the most famous in Spain. The *paso* of Our Lady of Sorrows advances amidst countless sparkling lights behind long lines of white-clad penitents, and perhaps the ardour roused in the city by political questions since the beginning of the nineteenth century may be found, in a very different manifestation, in the passionate beauty of Good Friday.

Now our journey takes us to the boundary between the Mediterranean and the Atlantic, to Gibraltar. So as to vary our itinerary we shall not drive along the sea but shall go to Ronda, one of the most picturesque towns of the far south of Andalusia. When we come from the station and go through the rectilinear suburbs we have no inkling of the grandiose surprise that awaits us on the bridge leading to the old city. Above a precipice more than 300 feet deep we can see through the railings of the parapet a sky-line of mountain between the houses perching on the slopes and a very low valley. We must cross the bridge and stroll along the old by-streets. Here and there houses attract us or a terrace reveals the distant horizon ; in front of the Santa Maria la Mayor Church, a mosque transformed after the Reconquest, a garden offers a peaceful spot. We must walk through the San Francisco district with its long streets disappearing mountainwards ; only the black gratings break the monotony of tones : the blue of the sky and the white of the houses. The far end of the district is also that of the long spur where Ronda held out against Ferdinand the Catholic until 1485. In the heart of Serrania, the city, perched on its lofty mountains, is indeed the capital of the legendary Andalusians whom we imagine as daring smugglers or famous bandits. And its true character — picturesque and grandiose — appears more distinctly as we leave the town and go down the slopes that descend in folds beneath its tall houses ; this town defies time just as it defied the Christians — and only the passage of a few flocks animates the silence of the valley as majestic as a frozen sea.

By way of the Sierra de Ronda and the Sierra Bermeja we shall go back to the shores of the Mediterranean ; after San Roque and La Linea we reach Gibraltar. The site might not have a moving grandeur — this peak planted here by Europe on the confines of its domain — yet it evokes so many centuries of history that it most certainly moves any traveller. What does it matter if the Greeks thought they could limit the horizons of the earth to this spot since two great events have taken place that have for ever influenced the destiny of Spain ! The Moslem invasion not only brought about several centuries of Reconquest but influenced the language, art and soul of the country, and the reaction imposed upon the Christians the common basis of their unity : the Catholic religion. And how important the capture of Gibraltar by the English in 1704 proved to be ! During the entire eighteenth century, by war or diplomacy, the Bourbon kings tried to recover this parcel of land torn away from the motherland and its memory remains a painful "thorn" implanted in its very heart. And these fleeting moments of meditation about its history are also those when we are amused to see, at a distance of a few hundred yards from traditional and picturesque Spain, a bit of eternal England, such as its soldiers and civil servants, sailors and colonists have taken pleasure in transporting to all parts of the earth. The houses, walks, customs, everything here breathes the atmosphere of the other side of the Channel and the superb rock resembles an aerolite torn away from the sky of Albion and fallen, by a sudden caprice of the

RONDA. THE TAJO.

THE ROCK OF GIBRALTAR.

gods, at the meeting-place of a sea and an ocean and of two continents.

Only the site of Algeciras, so near it on the other side of the gulf, is beautiful, and we shall drive quickly along the Atlantic whose breeze sometimes reaches us, cool and almost unexpected beneath the bright blue of the sky. We are at some distance from the coast, not far from Cape Trafalgar which gave its name to Nelson's last — and conclusive — victory.

ALGECIRAS. THE HARBOUR.

We pass on to the narrow spit of land connecting Cadiz to the mainland, and are greeted by an atmosphere almost like that of an African adventure : cacti, aloes, the sea breeze. But the salt-marshes with their pungent smell give the landscape its originality. Soon we see the whole bay and we comprehend its situation ; the spit of land at the tip of which stands Cadiz protects the built-up areas on the opposite shore from the open sea. These

SAN FERNANDO. THE SALT MARSHES.

NEAR CADIZ. THE HUERTA.

centres on the mainland are San Fernando, Puerto Real, the Trocadero, and Puerto de Santa Maria.

In some places, the passage-way between the ocean and the bay is only wide enough for the road and railway track ; our adventure at the tip of the continent is over ; we pass through the Puerta de Tierra, a vestige

CADIZ. GENOVES PARK.

CADIZ. THE FAÇADE OF THE CATHEDRAL.

of the eighteenth-century fortifications, and we find ourselves amid the bustle of the quays and the jolly symphony of colours of Cadiz. Spaniards call their city the *tacita de plata*, the little silver cup; to us it looks more like the long palm that Andalusia's capricious arm allows to float on the already far-distant waters of the ocean and that it carelessly holds; a sparkling bough of bright colours, white, green and blue, between sea and sky.

Let us drive all round the point on which the city is built. First we drive past the port where cargo-boats and liners put in as though it were the port of call of a happy island, then we pass the gardens that stretch along the ocean and whose flowers hide the entrance of the bay.

CADIZ MUSEUM. ZURBARAN. THE CARTHUSIAN CARDINAL, NICOLO ALBERGATI.

166

On the Alameda de Apodaca opens the church of Nuestra Señora del Carmen; it is all white with an almost plain façade, reserving its baroque exuberance for the upper part of the towers — and this baroque in a port, beneath this limpid sky, is all the more welcome as it recalls America and the expansion of the baroque style in the colonies. Near the fort of Santa Catalina we find ourselves at the very tip of the larger point which is Cadiz; the serene beauty of landscape and town seems so perfect that it would have been impossible, even in imagination, to create it; though there are few clouds, they make the brilliant sunlight more human; the sea breeze tempers the heat; it seems as though each day spent here prolongs what would be but un unforgettable hour in any other spot; an hour mingling the last moment of spring with the first of summer.

Now we walk along by the sea and we visit the old convent of Santa Catalina on our left. Near the silent patio whose great plants stand out against the spotless white arcades, the chapel houses some very fine paintings; the retable of the high altar consecrated to the mystical marriage of St. Catherine is Murillo's last work. While painting it in 1682 he fell from the platform and subsequently died.

The view of the ramparts, cathedral and ocean from the threshold of the old monastery is rightly called the *Campo de Mar* — field of the sea. A few houses, a rampart and the nearby ocean stretching to the horizon. The walk follows the sweep of the ramparts and disappears beneath the towers and cupola of the cathedral; behind, the houses add light spots here and there. We walk along the side and admire the façade; at first sight it seems rather overladen with decoration, but this eighteenth-century building, despite the heaviness of its Greco-Roman style, charms us by the breadth and harmony of its curved lines. Inside we admire a *St. Bruno* by Montañes, meditating before a skull, and the series of statues adorning the stalls.

Henceforth we wander at random through the regular streets of Cadiz; the Andalusian crowd throngs there in a setting that has a regularity not to be found in the other great towns of this region. That is, doubtless, one of the most striking characteristics of the city. In the same square as the cathedral is the house where Admiral Gravina died : he commanded the Spanish ships at Trafalgar and succumbed to his wounds after fighting like a hero; here is the church of Santiago; in a nearby square is the Ayuntamiento whose inscription recalls Cadiz's claims to glory. The city was the seat of the insurrectional *Junta* which directed the struggle against Napoleon; the Constitution which the Liberals were to quote as their authority in their subsequent struggles was proclaimed here in 1812 : the city took up their cause eagerly and Ferdinand VII, carried along by the Cortès in 1823, was only delivered by the arrival of the Duke of Angoulême at the head of a French army and the capture of the Trocadero.

The Oratory of San Felipe Neri, where the Cortès held their sessions from 1811 to 1812, possesses an *Immaculate Conception* by Murillo. The chapel of the Santa Cueva inside a decrepit house affords us an unusual surprise : several pictures by Goya — *The Last Supper, The Miracle of the Loaves and Fishes, The Guest Driven from the Wedding Feast* — adorn the concave surfaces of a chapel for which they were painted. The Fine Arts Museum is one of the richest to be found in the Spanish provinces. Without mentioning a goodly number of exceptional canvases, we shall only speak of one name — that of Zurbaran ; the portraits of monks which used to adorn the Carthusian monastery of Jerez are now divided between the museums of Grenoble and Cadiz — and this broken-up series at least deserves as much fame as that of Guadalupe which has been lucky enough to remain intact. Which one of these monks must we admire most ? Nicolas Albergati in ecstasy, wearing his broad-brimmed cardinal's hat ? John Houghton, with a rope round his neck, one hand on his heart and a prayer on his lips ? How graceful the censing angels are with their green corselets, pleated skirts and questioning look — and their rather affected charm ! Not far from these we might contemplate much bigger paintings : *St. Bruno in a Trance, The Portioncule.* But it is doubtless these angels, so pure and so feminine, that we inevitably remember.

On our way back to Seville, we do not lose sight of Zurbaran. Jerez de la Frontera offers us its splendid Carthusian monastery ; it is stripped of its paintings, but still has the rich setting they were made for. The traveller enters through a magnificent seventeenth-century door with superimposed orders. The city and its surroundings are famous for their wines and we may visit the cellars where the famous bottles are prepared.

Now the only thing left for us to see on the coast is the Huelva region from which we are separated by the Guadalquivir and which can only be reached from Seville. Thus we leave the coastal region taking away the memory of a Paradise Lost. On our way, isolated houses and whole villages shine forth against the red earth like bunches of white flowers, between cactus hedges, amidst tufts of aloes, and the sunlight is a luminous shower that admits of no shade.

INLAND

Is it possible to see without secret emotion Granada shimmering with light round its hills ? We were afraid it might not live up to our dream. But it is not a dream and when our expectations find themselves face to face with reality we are lost in a rapture we had never conceived. There is nothing artificial in its charm. Nature and men have created its many elements and to say that Granada is beautiful is merely to affirm their harmonious presence.

On the horizon the Sierra Nevada justifies its name by the snowy crown it proudly wears. The Darro — partly subterranean in the city —

THE SIERRA NEVADA.

waters it and enables the foliage and flowers to grow ; the Genil into which it flows ensures the irrigation of a rich *vega*. Granada itself, spread over a landscape which must have been splendid from the very beginning of time, has taken centuries to mould its face. The Alcazaba Cadina, the old fortress, stands on a hill which is now prolonged by the suburbs of the Albaicin ; at the bottom of the ravine flows the Darro and on the opposite height stands the Alhambra with the new Alcazaba, the palaces and enceinte ; not far outside the latter, a little mound bears the Torres Bermejas, thus named for their russet colour. Below spreads modern, contemporary Granada.

The city slowly emerged from obscurity as the power of Cordoba lessened. When the latter fell to the Christians in 1236 it became the capital of the one remaining Moslem State in the peninsula, from Gibraltar to Almeria, and from the sea to the source of the Guadalquivir. In 1238 Ibn El Ahmar founded the dynasty of the Nasrides who made the city a centre of art and science for two hundred and fifty years. They built the Alhambra and defended themselves fairly well against the irresistible Reconquest. But in the second half of the fifteenth century feuds in the royal family and rivalry between the Abencerrages and the Zegris occurred at a period when Christian Spain realized that the time had come to put an end to it. The Catholic Kings intensified the struggle and Boabdil, the last Moslem prince of Granada, besieged in his capital, handed it over to Ferdinand and Isabella on January 2, 1492. This is the most glorious date of all in Spanish history for it alone evokes the triumphant consummation of an epic struggle ; faith had won. And in the former capital of the Infidels, the Catholic Kings, abandoning their plan for St. John of the Kings in Toledo, desired to be buried on the very spot of the victory. Empress Isabella, Charles V's wife, lived there ; the Emperor had apartments installed there and undertook to build a classic palace near the Arab buildings. Yet in the city all during the sixteenth century *plateresco* and Renaissance buildings were erected. The revolt and expulsion of the Moors struck a terrible blow at the prosperity of the city and the region — to the entire economic system of the realm ; yet there are some splendid examples of the baroque period in Granada. But the Alhambra fell into disrepair. Chateaubriand, Roberts and travellers of the Romantic period imagined they had re-discovered the marvel and the poetic halo they set upon it has not yet vanished. Restoration has been slowly carried on and now we can once again enjoy the residence of the Moslem sovereigns.

So Granada is especially, but not wholly, the Alhambra, and the visit the traveller makes has more variety than he expected.

The centre of the present city lies at the end of the Carrera del Genil on the site of the old Puerta Real. Let us take the Calle de los Reyes Catolicos, one of the busiest streets ; we shall soon find the Casa del Carbon at the end of a wretched alley on our right. Its miserable appearance conceals a long history. Built by the Arabs in the fourteenth century, it became a theatre in the seventeenth. Not far from here, turned into a museum by the Tourist Office, stands the Casa de los Tiros, whose Renaissance façade is adorned with original sculptured figures. But let us go back to the Calle de los Reyes Catolicos. On our left we cross the narrow, picturesque streets of the former Arab bazaar, the "Alcaiceria" which, after being burnt down, was rebuilt to a similar plan in the nineteenth century.

We soon come out on to the Plazuela de las Pasiegas, charming on account of its conventual atmosphere rather than for the buildings around it ; the seventeenth-century episcopal palace, the main façade of the cathedral dating from the same period, the least interesting part of the building. Begun in 1521 by Enrique de Egas, carried on by Diego de Siloé whose masterpiece it was (1528-1563), continued in the seventeenth and finished during the first years of the eighteenth century, it attracts us by the limpid majesty of the whole, by the Renaissance decoration which predominates, except for the crownings, on the Perdon and San Jeronimo doors — it dazzles us by the splendour of its *capilla mayor* — it holds our attention by the beauty of the *capilla real* built to house the tombs of the Catholic Kings. This last opens on to the south side of the transept. Around four royal tombs — the recumbent effigies of Philip the Handsome and Joanna the Madwoman on a second plinth beside those of their parents — we utter the names of wonderful artists at each step : Enrique de Egas, the architect, Domenico Fancelli, for the tombs of the Catholic Kings, Bartolomé Ordoñez for those of their daughter and son-in-law, Bartolomé de Jaen for the main gate, Philip Vigarny for the retable of the high altar, and the triptych portraying the *Descent from the Cross* is by Memling... But here art should only furnish the setting for our meditations. The glory of the conquerors of Granada, the long years of madness of their daughter entrapped in her tragic jealousy and the premature death of Philip the Handsome... The sacristy of the chapel contains the sceptre, sword and chest of the Catholic Kings — and a collection of Flemish paintings which forms an intimate and exceptional museum.

The *plateresco* decoration of the outside door of the chapel forms a contrast with the neighbouring façade : the Casa del Cabildo Antiguo — a vestige of the Arab university — has a strange eighteenth-century front.

How many other buildings dating from the sixteenth to the eighteenth centuries could we find in Granada ! Renaissance or *plateresco* art flourish at the Audiencia with a remarkable patio, or at Santa Ana's church, or above all at that of San Jeronimo : the sanctuary is no longer used for divine service, the silence is not that of meditation but of abandonment, and the tombs of the Gran Capitan and his wife are the object of an indifference they could never have wished for in their life-time.

The San Juan de Dios hospital has a rather over-decorated baroque chapel — but what can be said of the sacristy of the Carthusian monastery !

GRANADA. THE ALHAMBRA. THE LADIES' TOWER.

GRANADA. THE COURTYARD OF THE LIONS IN THE ALHAMBRA.

Heavy with marble, furnished with ebony, tortoise-shell and silver, with a multiplicity of curves, it is beautiful through the very profusion of its decoration — but so little suited to be a sacristy (and in a convent); before and after their office it welcomes the most ascetic monks in Christendom as if they were opera-singers.

In 1238, a few months after the capture of Granada, Ibn Al Ahmar began building the new Alcazaba which was perhaps continued by his son Mohammed II (1273-1302) and it is doubtless to them and their immediate successors that we owe part of the towers and the enceinte; but the palaces they built disappeared and were replaced by those which are standing today. Yusuf I (1333-1354) built different towers of the Casa Real or Alcazar (this is the name given to the group of royal dwellings) of the enceinte, and the Royal Baths; Mohammed V (1354-1391) ordered the rest to be built. The transformations made by the Catholic Kings are negligible but those made by Charles V are important. Such as it is today, despite the ravages of time, the Alhambra is undoubtedly the most beautiful Arab palace we can admire.

We leave the modern city by way of the Puerta de las Granadas, and this Renaissance gate by Pedro Machuca with its excessive bossages affords us an unexpected entrance. Then we go up a very shady road which gives an impression of mystery and poetry, but we must not attribute their presence to the builders of the Alhambra; it was a fortress and as such demanded an open approach. A few yards further on, we are welcomed by the cool murmur of a fountain, the Pilar de Carlos Quinto, in the same classical style and by the same artist as the entrance gate. A few steps more and we at last find Arab art as we pass beneath the noble and majestic brick arch of the Puerta de la Justicia; a polychrome Virgin, ordered by the Catholic Kings, already indicates that the Christian sovereigns and faith had taken possession of the Alhambra. After the Puerta del Vino, a doorway in the second enceinte, we come out on to the Plaza de los Algibes (or cisterns), a huge, open space between the Alcazaba on the left, Charles the Fifth's palace and the Alcazar of the Moslem princes on the right; the view of the Albaicin and of the ravine of the Darro spreads before us in the background. Actually the site has been disfigured; the moat that used to protect the Alcazaba was turned into a cistern by Ferdinand and Isabella and when Charles V's palace was built, they did away with the buildings which normally led up to the Alcazar to make room for a huge parade-ground.

The Alcazaba is completely independent of the Alhambra, their only common feature being the enceinte, which has a triangular shape, and we are at the point of the height where the buildings spread out. Inside the enceinte rise the towers and ramparts belonging to the Alcazaba alone; up that of the Vela, Cardinal Mendoza, the count of Tendilla, the Master of Santiago and other notables climbed, on January 2, 1492, to raise the sign of the Cross, the emblem of Santiago, and the Royal Standards there while the Catholic Kings watched them from below... Between the enceinte and the ramparts stretches the Garden of Los Adarves, full of greenery and facing an admirable panorama.

What a contrast there is between the palace that the European Charles V had Pedro Machuca build for him and the surrounding buildings. Its circular courtyard produces a very harmonious impression and seems more original than it may actually be for the architect did little more than carry out a rather usual Italian idea. But to the visitor from the Alcazar who suddenly comes out into the courtyard, it seems that the sky changes and that the music of the air is no longer the same. The outer façades are majestically revealed according to the canons of pure, classical architecture.

We enter the Alcazar and go from marvel to marvel. We should mingle the memory of the Arab kings with the artistic explanation and the poetic incantation. We are completely out of our element ; contrary to our palaces, there is no pre-conceived plan here, no leading idea ; the rooms were juxtaposed or superposed as the necessity arose throughout the fourteenth century which witnessed the arranging of most of them. The prince held his audiences in the Mexuar ; behind it, an oratory keeps in store for us the surprise of its delicate arches and exquisite indentations. The Cuarto de Comares includes the famous Courtyard of Myrtles, the Hall of La Barca and that of the Ambassadors. On the shorter sides of the patio rise seven arches whose monotony is broken by the central one which is taller than the others ; the smooth walls of the longer sides recede and are scarcely broken by the irregular doors and windows ; between the two lines of archways spreads the calm water of the pool over which eternity seems to hover. In the Hall of La Barca we admire the white marble niches ; then we enter the Hall of the Ambassadors. It is a perfect square, lighted on three sides by windows with balconies, a few of them geminated ; the deep recesses of the windows form little rooms with an admirable view over the gardens of the Generalife and the ravine of the Darro. Doubtless the royal throne used to stand in a recess opposite the entrance. Here Boabdil took leave of his family and friends before the battles that were to end with the fall of Granada. Beautiful as this hall seems to us today with its delicate decoration, its vast size and view, how different it is from its former state ; the bright colours used to sparkle, the windows must have been glazed with stained glass, princes used to live there in all their splendour !

Now we are walking through the Baño Real, whose slender white marble columns mark the limit of a central square between narrow passageways, and the Torre del Peinador. From this tower, doubtless partly converted for the Empress Isabella who never used it, the view plunges over the valley. Between the Cuarto de Comares, the Baño Real and the Peinador de la Reina stretch the Garden of Daraxa and the apartments

175

GRANADA. THE ALHAMBRA. THE HALL OF KINGS.

prepared for Charles the Fifth; there Washington Irving wrote his *Tales of the Alhambra*. But the most attractive spot is the small patio — rather ironically, it does not date from the Arab period, but from the seventeenth century — that of the Reja whose cypresses, foliage and water make us linger long.

And the Courtyard of the Lions appears — edged with wonderful rooms. The elegance of the arches reaches such a degree of refinement that after seeing this masterpiece, we cannot conceive of any other possibility but that of repetition or decline. The temples adorning the shorter sides keep the galleries from becoming monotonous. How many pictures have portrayed this courtyard all over the world. Yet one can spend several days in Granada and return to it constantly; it is ever new and perfect.

The hall of the Two Sisters takes its name from two similar slabs of white marble, and that of the Abencerrages from the supposed execution of the members of this family. But even if we ignored their names we should be quite content to dream amidst the stucco work and painted tiles; near us stands the vase of the Alhambra, an admirable specimen of Hispano-Moresque ceramics; it evokes all those that formerly decorated these silent rooms and that have now disappeared. Finally the Hall of Kings contains fourteenth-century paintings on leather : their western character is very curious; they represent ten figures which have been thought to be kings, hence the name of the room. But we cannot tear our eyes from the vault and arches with an effect of stalactites.

The marvellous whole formed by these palaces is surrounded by gardens and towers. The elegant façade of the Torre del Damas — which must not be mistaken for the towers of the enceinte — is mirrored in a pool before rising prospects of foliage and flowers.

It is opposite the Alhambra, in the Generalife, that we must admire the perfection of the garden. It is the only one left of all the residences where the Moslem princes used to seek rest and solitude. Its characteristics are essentially Arabian : fruit-trees and flowers are juxtaposed, the terrain is divided up instead of affording sweeping vistas. The Generalife ? It is the song of the fountains, the Alhambra seen through quivering foliage; it is the Patio de la Acequia, lying between two pavilions, and that of the cypresses, meditating between the trees and water. How can we speak of it without enumerating its charms one by one ? It is, precisely an atmosphere and a landscape, the peace of a dream one lives amidst the branches and musical fountains.

A distant murmur rises towards the Alhambra, that of the districts that spread along the ravine of the Darro; there are many churches and beautiful houses there. We must stroll through it and go as far as the gypsy district — unfortunately too well-known — for the dances and costumes shown to the tourists in the Albaicin or at the Sacro Monte have lost much of their zest. But an exceptionally beautiful woman sometimes appears and this makes up for all our disillusion. In the day-time only gypsies walk on the slopes of the Sacro Monte, all white and riddled with wretched dwellings ; yet how beautiful the view is ! The lines are clear cut, the city quivers in the distance, the Alhambra unfolds its series of towers, the bright sunlight continues to flood the scene.

Yet the evening imperceptibly softens the sunshine, twilight falls, the Alhambra falls back into the silence which has been its very soul for so many centuries and whose surface only is troubled by visitors for a few short hours ; the murmur of the gypsy quarter increases, its caves become light-filled holes, travellers are enraptured by their dances.

Night quickly passes and with it the ephemeral life of the Sacro Monte comes to an end. Soon day returns and as is the case every morning the sun re-invents the light of Granada — and we who are leaving are sure of never exhausting the delight of its memory.

Towards Jaen, about sixty miles away, the beauty of the road comes from the barrenness of a depopulated countryside — we pass through a single village — and the splendour of the mountain ranges ; we must cross two passes and the Sierra de Alta Coloma. The city itself is confined and hilly. The cathedral, where a famous relic of the Holy Face is worshipped, is a huge edifice built to Vandelvira's plans between the sixteenth and eighteenth centuries ; the main façade between two tall towers has a multiplicity of columns, pilasters, windows and gables. So much pomp and grandeur form a strange contrast to the rest of the city. It is because the general impression produced by Jaen gave promise of a quite different building. The town is built on a mountain site, the narrow streets form a complicated maze, the wind often blows a gale ; the alleys of the old Arab quarter stretch interminably as far as the castle, and when it has rained hard or if the wind is blowing, the water as it disappears into the narrow thoroughfares of this district, carries along reddish earth which looks like tainted blood.

The retables of San José's church attracted us with their picturesque simplicity and their violence ; in this one, the naked souls in torment are writhing in the flames, in that one St. Ildefonse's life is told. Isn't the presence of majestic cathedrals in the most unexpected towns one of Spain's charms ? The twin cities of Baeza and Ubeda, separated by some eight miles, remind us of Salamanca with their ochre-colour, the style of their *plateresco*, Renaissance or baroque edifices which are equally golden and elegant — and if the majesty of Salamanca is lacking, they lie in a mountainous landscape which it lacks.

From the main square of Baeza, we go to San Andrès' church ; its portal and the top of the square tower have delicate sculpture to show us. The ruins of the convent of San Francisco, the Ayuntamiento and the seminary of San Felipe are other halts during our delightful walk, and the cathedral still lies in store for us... But the pleasantest moment is the one

GRANADA CATHEDRAL. THE CAPILLA REAL. THE TOMB OF PHILIP THE HANDSOME
AND JOANNA THE MADWOMAN BY BART. ORDONEZ.

GRANADA. FLOWERED BALCONIES IN THE ALBAICIN.

GRANADA. AT THE SACRO MONTE.

BAEZA. SORTING GRAIN.

UBEDA. PALACE OF LOS ORTEGAS.

when we commence an aimless stroll : we discover a palace ; we notice details of a building which had escaped us, and we feast our eyes on the light playing on the carved stone-work and the sculptures of the porches...

To go to Ubeda, we leave aside the blue or white villages whose tiered houses stand out on the mountainside ; the air is limpid, the light seems

JAEN. GENERAL VIEW AND CATHEDRAL.

to caress the lines of the landscape, unwilling to tolerate anything but a
strong and harmonious beauty everywhere.

The artistic centre of the city is Vazquez de Molina Square, edged

184

THE ROOFS OF CORDOBA SEEN FROM THE TOP OF THE MOSQUE.

CORDOBA. INSIDE THE MOSQUE.

with several palaces and two churches. Santa Maria de los Reales Alcazares was a mosque before the Reconquest and still has its five original naves later covered by sham vaults. Doubtless the main façade, redone in the seventeenth century, has no very good sculpture to offer us, but it is noteworthy for the rhythm of the belfries framing the portico. Inside, the grilles by Bartolomé de Jaen — who forged that of the *capilla real* of Granada, as we know — possess the evocative strength that we did not expect to find in the material used or in the limited number of figures or in such a confined space. It is the meeting of Joachim and Elizabeth, it is the story of Adam and Eve ; naked they stand round the tree where the serpent is coiled, the Angel flies up and drives them out of Paradise. How can these few figures, as they stand out against emptiness, move us to such a degree?

The jewel of Ubeda is the church of the Salvador, built from 1540 to 1556 by Andrès de Vandelvira according to Diego de Siloé's plans. What charm there is in the two storeys of the portico of the façade giving on to the square. Its decoration was inspired by the Puerta del Perdon of Granada's cathedral and it can stand the comparison. The delicate grace of the south portal, the originality of the Puerta de la Paz which stands in an angle and forms an inside passage from the sanctuary to the sacristy ! The holy characters and profane figures, naked women and draped caryatides are arranged in a merry harmony. We imagine that we can feel in these statues the pleasure felt by the artists who were using a newly discovered language, improving the form of a recumbent woman, multiplying the rose-windows and garlands : everything here is new, free and happy. In the church behind a grating forged in Toledo, the *Transfiguration of Christ* is by Alonso Berruguete ; around it the golden tide of baroque decoration unfolds with its usual superabundance.

How many palaces, how many churches Ubeda could still reveal to us : San Nicolas, San Pablo and their admirable grilles, the Casa de las Torres and its majestically smiling façade ! The narrow streets stretch away, studded with coats of arms on the noble façades.

And just imagine Good Friday within these walls, when the *pasos* leave the trains of the Virgins, spangled with gold, behind them amidst the countless lights.

Ubeda has a grave elegance ; the human gravity which is the very stamp of aristocracy.

***

Now we are going to Cordoba by way of the industrial city of Linarès and we come back to the Madrid road at Bailen, so sadly famous for the capitulation of General Dupont in 1809, which rang the knell for Napoleon's successes in Spain. Andujar is a picturesque old town from which we can go to the sanctuary of the Virgin de la Cabeza ; during the Civil War, it was held by a few besieged nationalists for months and their resistance is one of the most famous episodes in that terrible struggle.

Henceforth, until we get to Cordoba, we go down along the Guadalquivir; on the vast tablelands, ploughed fields, olive-trees and holm-oaks are mingled.

"Cordoba", wrote Théophile Gautier, "looks more African than any other town in Andalusia; its streets or rather its alleys, whose tumultuous pavements look like the beds of dried-up mountain streams, are littered with short straw that has fallen from donkeys' loads, have nothing that reminds us of the customs or habits of Europe. You walk between interminable chalk-coloured walls with a few windows here and there covered with gratings and bars and you only meet some beggar with a forbidding face, some black-hooded church-goer or a *majo* flashing by on his white-saddled brown horse, as thousands of sparks fly up from the flints of the paved road. If the Moors could come back, they would have little to do to settle here once again."

Of course some details of this description would have to be changed, but the impression it conveys is still exact today for one whole district, the one that corresponds to the ancient city and stretches from the Guadalquivir to the beginning of the Avenida del Gran Capitan; it takes in the mosque, old churches, typical streets and generally the interesting public buildings.

Cordoba became one of the capitals of Islam at the very beginning of the Arab domination and in 756 Abd Er Rhaman shook off the yoke of the caliph of Damascus and took the title of Emir. He and his successors brought fame and prosperity to the city, they built the *mezquita* or mosque which has become the cathedral. But the battle of Las Navas de Tolosa (1212) ruined Moslem power in the region and St. Ferdinand made his entrance into the city. Its decline then began: it was too near its former masters and feared their raids; the Christians let its industry dwindle and abandoned the irrigation work. It has hardly recovered yet from this decline, but the old quarters still have their picturesque aspects made even more moving by a certain dilapidation; the modern avenues have been laid out elsewhere.

What irreplaceable things can the traveller find here? The collection of medieval churches, the most beautiful of which is San Pablo. The synagogue dating from 1314, the palaces and ordinary houses, the total effect of the old city near the cathedral and the *mezquita* itself.

We go down towards it by way of the confined district which used to abound in the picturesque in Théophile Gautier's days. We must catch a glimpse, framed by the gates, of the interiors of the houses, and a peep at the foliage within the patios and at the bright spots of the *azulejos*. The streets intersect and form a true maze: sometimes we take a by-way to get a better view of a door or of some flowers, sometimes the street suddenly

188

CORDOBA CATHEDRAL. THE MAKSURAH.

widens into a little square immediately flooded with sunlight; the bright-coloured plants on the rough white plaster walls shout their blaze but are as fresh to the eye as a breath of air. The *mezquita* looms in front of us while we are still under the spell of the network of alleys. We walk round its dilapidated walls whose sadness wrings the heart. How far off the century when the mosque was gloriously new and opulent! Now it seems as though its architecture and decoration were simply a grey print of its former splendour.

Abd Er Rhaman, not content with having ensured its independence, wanted to build the finest mosque in Islam in his capital. The edifice was begun in 785 and continued by Hisham I; it had eleven naves. It was first enlarged towards the south by Abd Er Rhaman II in 833 and 848 according to the same principles and with the same depth; it was enlarged for the second time and again southwards and still with the same depth by Hachem II (961-966); finally El Mansour lengthened all the naves eastwards and considerably increased the depth itself (987-990). As it was then, the *mezquita* had nineteen naves whose details differed according to the period but they produced a uniform impression and were prolonged in the Patio de los Naranjos by verdant walks. Just think of the lustre of the marble, of the light coming in through the archways opening on to the outside world (today the cathedral is terribly dark compared to the mosque) and turning, as it were, into arches of orange-trees through which the sunlight filtered here and there.

After the Reconquest, the naves were closed off on the patio side, chapels were arranged, and the *mezquita* became a cathedral. But the sixteenth-century chapter undertook the erection of a new cathedral built in the style of the day in the centre of the old building. Despite the opposition and Charles the Fifth himself the building went on; with its huge stone cross, it towers above the harmonious profusion of columns giving the impression that a heavy mass has fallen upon a forest and that the lives of both buildings follow different rhythms, in a state of perpetual hostility. In the wall surrounding the Patio de los Naranjos rises the Puerta del Perdon; its style is Moresque, but it dates from the fourteenth century and is partly in ruins now. On leaving the Tour del Alminar rebuilt in the sixteenth and seventeenth centuries, we enter the Patio, where long rows of orange-trees give us promise of rest. We have but to take a few steps amidst this greenery to fall under the spell; in our imagination and our hearts, we find the *mezquita* as it was of yore. We enter and are quite bewildered and confused for we only see, disappearing in all directions, arches and groups of columns of a rare beauty; we are reminded of the infinite for we have the impression that no centre exists here; we see only columns, such beautiful columns that this cannot be an earthly dwelling. We imagine "that we are walking in a high-ceilinged forest rather than in a building", Théophile Gautier also said. "Wherever you look, your eyes wonder along alleys of columns which intercross and stretch away as far as the eye can see like a kind of marble vegetation that has suddenly sprung up out of the ground ; the mysterious half-light prevailing in this wood makes the illusion even more complete..." We must walk there and admire the different capitals and the superposed tiers of arches. Ironically enough, the passage of time has made the *mihrab* so dark that we cannot see the marvellously scalloped arcades, the arabesques and mosaics. The sexton has to pass an electric lamp hanging from a wire here and there to bring all this splendour out of the shadows ; an impression of magical opulence is given by this lighting now too harsh, now too dim.

The sixteenth-century cathedral is not lacking in merit — but how can we appreciate it rightly within this mosque that it disfigures ?

On leaving the building, we once again grow sad on seeing the outside walls whose splendour has been mercilessly destroyed by time and neglect. Let us go down towards the Roman bridge and cross the river ; it is the other bank that will leave us with the most moving memory of Cordoba : the yellowish waters of the Guadalquivir, near the battlements and machicol-ations of the Calahorra, opposite us the Puerta del Puente dating from the days of Philip II and behind it, with the Alcazar on the left, the *mezquita*, a mass that can never be submerged either by floods or time.

* * *

Sevilla es una torre
llena de arqueros finos.
Sevilla para herir
Cordoba para morir...

This poem by Garcia Lorca, or rather this incantation alternating between Cordoba the mortal and Seville which wounds with its intoxi-cation, is what we repeat to ourselves along the road leading to the capital of Andalusia across the monotonous countryside.

Die in Cordoba ? To be sure, but the ardent mystery of its joy draws us on towards Seville, the city triumphant, gay, white and flowery beneath the sky.

The little towns that precede it are merely a picturesque repetition of the city itself ; Ecija, rich in churches and palaces, Carmona, where the tower of San Pedro looms up like a Giralda of its own. The landscape along the Guadalquivir disappears in the direction of the marvellous city without affording any feature that really catches the eye, and the light which around us glares mercilessly on the olive-trees, ploughed fields or lagoons, we imagine it, we feel it as it must be in Seville when it brings out the vast surfaces of the spotless walls.

The Moors captured the city in 712 and it quickly grew as important as Cordoba. The Almohades built public buildings, some of which still

CORDOBA. THE PLAZA DE LAS FLORES.

CORDOBA. THE CASA DE DON GOMEZ.

exist : the Tower of Gold and part of the Alcazar. After the battle of Las Navas de Tolosa, the Moslem hold over the city was broken and St. Ferdinand made his entrance in 1248. Alfonso the Wise and Peter the Cruel resided here. Great discoveries and trade with America brought it an unheard-of prosperity. It was not only materially wealthy but it also had an abundance of artists ; its school of painting enjoyed a period of constant splendour : Pacheco, Velazquez, Murillo, Herrera el Viejo, Herrera el Mozo, his son, were born within its walls. Cervantes had set many episodes of the *Exemplary Short Stories* in Seville ; *Rinconete and Cortadillo* is a literarily perfect description of the picturesque, engaging underworld of this booming town.

Today it is the capital of the south of Spain, the city of the flamenco and other dances, of patios full of foliage and adorned with *azulejos* ; it is pre-eminently the city of the Holy Week and the *Feria* towards which tourists flock in search of a picturesque atmosphere that their very presence tends to spoil.

We shall begin our visit in the centre of the town, bustling with heavy traffic and lined with cafés and shops. After the Campana circus we enter the narrow Calle de las Sierpes, where cars cannot drive and pedestrians throng between the light walls ; in the strip of sky bounded by the houses we find the sky of Andalusia again.

At the far end, in the centre of two huge squares, one of them that of San Fernando, stands the Renaissance Ayuntamiento restored in the nineteenth century ; it forms a rather majestic whole and has a beautiful *plateresco* wing. Beyond it we reach the Puerta del Perdon which does not open into the cathedral itself but into the patio preceding it.

Begun in 1402, finished in the sixteenth century, constantly enriched with works of art since then, it is one of the most majestic and charming Spanish cathedrals because of its manifold aspects. After the Reconquest, Ferdinand III had transformed the mosque into a cathedral under the invocation of the Virgin.

But the assaults of time and earthquakes made such a ruin of the building that in 1401 the chapter decided to have a new church built by the most famous architects, and it is said that a canon on leaving the meeting exclaimed : "Let us build so big a church that those who see it completely finished will consider us madmen !"

And indeed the cathedral is huge ; seen from the Plaza del Triumfo, or from the square of the archiepiscopal palace, it looks like a monstrous yet ethereal hull that has run aground on the banks of the Guadalquivir, eager to set sail again for a divine sea. But it still has, in an indefinable way, the nostalgic aspect of a mosque. Of the latter there remains the Puerta del Perdon, the Patio de las Naranjos, harmonious and fragrant, and the Giralda, so beautiful and famous that it has become the very symbol of Seville ; its top was transformed in the sixteenth century but it is still possible to repeat the words of the Arab chronicler who knew it when it was the great minaret of the mosque and who exclaimed: "It has the same aspect, seen a day's walk from Seville, as the stars of the Zodiac". It is the splendid legacy left by Abu-Jacob and his son Abu-Yusuf to the reconquered city.

The sculpture on the portals is of unequal quality; we must admire, on the main front, the statues of San Juan and San Miguel, and on the east side the doors of Las Campanillas and Los Pallos.

But we shall linger longer before the incredible collection of artistic treasures inside.

Under the admirable vaults, the *capilla mayor*, decorated in the sixteenth century, seems to have rejected all that was not grandiose : the gates by Fray Francisco of Salamanca ; the scenes from the life of Christ, the Virgin and the Sevillan saints forming the retables — which appear of equal height to the person who gazes at them from the ground — and the altar placed under the protection of the sixteenth-century Virgen de la Sede.

What a quantity of Virgins this sanctuary contains !

It is impossible for us to speak of each of them and we must be content with the most beautiful chapels, the finest objects. The *capilla real* tells, as it were, the story of the devotion to St. Ferdinand beneath its Renaissance vaults : here is the shrine that Philip V gave to contain his body ; here is the statuette of the Virgen de los Reyes, that St. Louis is supposed to have given his cousin ; here the ivory Virgen de las Batallas, that he is supposed to have carried on his saddle-bow.

As we go from chapel to chapel and from one part to another, we should describe the gold plate, paintings, retables and liturgical ornaments. The great altar curtains by Juan de Arfe pile up their circular tiers adorned with multiple columns.

Zurbaran's *St. Peter* clasps his hands and turns an imploring face skywards. Murillo's *St. Francis of Assisi* is in ecstasy before the Christ Child appearing in a cloud within a crown of angels ; his *St. Isidorus*, the great bishop of Seville, meditates as he reads a book, holding his crosier and wearing his mitre. He is almost as fine as one of Zurbaran's monks. St. Justus and St. Rufina, holding palms in their hands and looking at the sky, show us a rather unexpected religious aspect of Goya. Pedro de Campana's *Descent from the Cross* (a painter of Flemish origin) reveals an artist of unsuspected merit.

What can we say about the sculpture that prepares us for the popular works of the *pasos* ?

Montañés's *Christo de la Clemencia*, sagging under the weight of distended arms ; Pedro de Mena's *Dolorosa*, clad in sumptuous garments, weeps, the regular-featured face inclined forward.

The great adventure of Spain is present, thanks to the funeral monuments of Christopher Columbus in the transept and of his son in front of the Puerta Mayor. Near the latter, a wooden structure with four

SEVILLE CATHEDRAL. THE PATIO DE LOS NARANJOS SEEN FROM THE GIRALDA.

SEVILLE. THE GIRALDA.

tiers is set up during Holy Week and the sight of the lamps burning round
it is an unforgettable spectacle.

This cathedral, which witnesses every year the solemn procession
of the Penitents accompanying the chariots of Christ and the Virgin,

belonging to their brotherhood, has an even rarer privilege : the ceremony called the *baile de los Seises*. It seems to date back to the period when the faithful desired to venerate the Blessed Sacrament by conforming, to the letter, to the terms of Urban IV's bull. In any case, today it is the religious dance of ten little singers, dressed as pages, who sing and dance in honour of the Eucharist and the Virgin in front of the Blessed Sacrament, accompanied by musical instruments. Thus, in its most venerable sanctuary, Seville keeps up the age-old union of dancing, singing and sacred worship.

On leaving the cathedral, we go by the sixteenth-century building called La Lonja where the *Archivo de Indias* is housed, that is to say the whole collection of documents concerning Spanish America, and a few steps further we shall enter the Alcazar.

The Arabs had built a castle on the site but the building as we now see it, is above all the work of Peter the Cruel who converted and decorated it in the fourteenth century though it has often been altered since then. We are extremely disappointed by it after visiting the Alhambra which has a better situation, is much bigger and has a purer and more evocative style. The decoration of some of the work that Peter the Cruel entrusted to Moorish artists is attractive but the restorations have not always sufficiently respected it. The Patio de las Doncellas, the drawing-room of the Ambassadors, and the Patio de la Munecas abound in delicate indentations and arches which remind us of Granada.

The *azulejos* of the Alcazar are very beautiful in the Oratory of the Catholic Kings adorned with a *Visitation* in the Italian style by Francisco Niculoso. The memory of Maria di Padilla and Peter the Cruel still hovers over the palace ; a feeling of tranquillity and poetry prevails in the shady flower gardens.

The Barrio de Santa Cruz is the most enchanting part of Seville. Its network of white alleys, so spotlessly clean, offers us little squares where oranges seem to blaze against the background of dark green leaves, where fountains play in the shadows a few yards from houses suffused with light ; above, plants form a leafy arch, and through the gates we can see cool, intimate patios. Murillo's house adds an artistic charm to our delightful walk.

Near the cathedral are two hospitals, that of the "Venerables" or Old Priests, which has some remarkable paintings, and that of La Caridad founded by Don Miguel de Mañara, who was first a brave gentleman famous for his valorous deeds and love affairs, and who then became a godly man known for his heroic charity ; legends have made him the prototype of Don Juan. His tomb consists of a plain slab placed at the entrance of the chapel. He wanted all those who entered it to tread upon his wretched body. The slab has remained but the mortal remains of the founder have been transferred to the sanctuary. There is hardly a chapel anywhere that has such a collection of famous pictures, painted on the very spot where we admire them. Murillo painted the *Miracle of the Loaves and Fishes* and the episode of *Moses striking the Rock;* Valdès Leal the famous picture in which the open coffins of the archbishop and the knight are overrun with worms [1].

Now we go along the embankments of the Guadalquivir and we walk through the gardens : Maria Louisa's or those near San Telmo's palace, built in the seventeenth and eighteenth centuries and adorned with a Churrigueresque door. The building, now a seminary, belonged to the Duke of Montpensier, the son of Louis-Philippe ; after marrying Isabella II's younger sister, he spent his life in Spain. The thirteenth century Tower of Gold built on the bank of the river, goes back to the Almohades' period. Let us walk on for quite a distance and enter the quiet streets which are one of the charms of Seville : irregular, edged with white houses, brightened by flowers that pass through the black wrought-iron gates, they lead us to the Fine Arts Museum.

Its collections, installed around two patios, contain many works by Valdès Leal, Murillo and Zurbaran. The first of the trio has little effect upon us and this may be rather unjust. The second often yields to a sentimentality which no longer corresponds to our standards, but certain works class him among the greatest painters, for instance : *St. Thomas of Villanueva assisting the Poor.* Zurbaran has an inimitable serious charm when he presents to us St. Inès dressed in flowing robes and holding a lamb in her arms. He was the painter of monks and it is their faces that we look for in the difficult pictures he ventured to paint, in the *Conference between Urban II and St. Bruno*, in the *Apotheosis of St. Thomas Aquinas*. And who can forget, after seeing them once, *St. Dorothea and St. Marina*, Inès's charming sisters ? The *Virgen de las Cuevas*, spreading the folds of her mantle over the kneeling Carthusian monks ? Or St. Hugh and the Carthusian monks in the dining-hall ?

Now we go from church to church, from palace to palace, here looking for the sculpture which expresses the popular faith of Seville, there for patios with their stately archways and multicoloured *azulejos*. Among the finest creations dating from the end of the fifteenth century and the sixteenth is the so-called : "Casa de Pilatos" as well as the house of the Duke of Alba. Here we evoke all the intimate life of Seville seen in the beauty of its own setting far from the stifling heat that prevails outside. Man flees from the street flooded by summer sunlight and takes refuge among the coolness of the plants.

---

(1) Commenting on this picture, Montherlant interpreted the inscription *Ni mas ni menos* above the scales of Vices and Virtues as being intentionally Machiavellian and perfidiously anti-Catholic. Is it not rather an excessive effect, so common in Spain with its fundamental belief in the emptiness of human greatness, applied to a well-known point of the Christian doctrine : without the grace that, at the origin of all spiritual life, God alone can grant the soul, all that man does — good or evil, — is null and void ?

SEVILLE. THE GARDENS OF THE ALCAZAR.

SEVILLE. THE ALCAZAR : THE AMBASSADORS' DRAWING ROOM.

Sevilla, the ardent city, reaches its paroxysm during the *Feria* and Holy week.

During these days, at the Prado of San Sebastien, the *Feria* animates the city with a gaiety which is not at all religious. In the wooden and canvas *casetas*, into which the passers-by can look, people dance and sing, and each great family sets its heart on getting its *caseta*. Then the smart festivities take place, couples on horseback peacock about the streets and Seville enjoys magnificent nights. Yet the bull-fighting season in the *plaza* attracts throngs of people and the most famous matadors.

Here, Holy Week is everybody's concern. In the suburbs, that of Triana on the other bank of the river vies with the worshippers of the Virgin from San Gil, near the Macarena Gate. And some of the Sevillans passionately sing the praises of the "Virgin of Triana" while the others do the same for the "Virgin of La Macarena".

The rhythm of life in the city changes, and it takes on an unforgettable beauty. It is not austere piety but a prodigious overflow of benevolence. Christ, even during the most tragic moments of his earthly existence, remains very close to the people of Seville, who honour him with the temperament that Heaven has given them. Some enrol themselves in the brotherhoods of penitents, the *nazarenos*; others burst into *saetas* as the *pasos* go by; still others organize rows of chairs in the main streets and rent them for high prices; finally, many of them make up the crowd which throngs by and applauds the Virgin they side with. They may suddenly kneel, caught up in a moving outburst of devotion. The aspect of the streets is that of a popular holiday but their hearts overflow with piety and there are gravely impressive moments.

During the first days of Holy Week, all the brotherhoods of penitents go from their churches to the cathedral, forming processions around their *pasos*; as a rule there are two. One must represent Our Lady of Sorrows, a *Dolorosa*, the other, Christ at some time during the Passion. These statues express popular art and the faith of the artists, particularly in the seventeenth and eighteenth centuries, to the highest degree. The sculpture must imitate reality, the sorrow of the holy figures must be flagrant and call forth cries. Though our French conception of art is very far from theirs, artists like Montañès and Ruiz Gijon, reach a degree of incontestable beauty. The faithful add costly garments to these poignant images; the Virgins, above all, are crowned with diadems and their immense trains look like gold carpets studded with diamonds.

The brotherhoods march in a set order. The cross, oriflammes and the standard head the procession; then come the hooded penitents clad in black, white or still other colours, using tall, lighted tapers as sticks, and finally the two *pasos*. The latter are borne by common labourers, the *costaleros* who are concealed by the tapestries hanging from the floor of the chariot and see nothing of what goes on outside. The whole weight rests on the nape of the neck, which they carefully cover with a bag. In the cafés near the starting-points you may speak with some of them and learn their impressions over a glass of *manzanilla*. Their invisible advance is guided by the *capataz*, who, with the help of many ejaculations as he walks backwards, directs their difficult progress. As the *paso* rests on their necks they advance very slowly, halting often. The most difficult moments are the departure from the church and the return. Often the door is hardly any wider than the *paso*, and the bearers, sitting on the floor almost, brush the ground, creating a murmur that reaches the ears of the onlookers through the singing of the *saetas*. Throughout the week we harvest moments of purity — those when religious emotion, the beauty and picturesque aspect of the scene hold our attention. On Palm Sunday, in the afternoon, a brotherhood leaves San Juan de las Palmas ; the crowd, all a-quiver with emotion, has invaded the little square ; the *nazarenos* advance as a *paso* appears, and one after the other the *saetas* burst forth from the balconies while overhead, in an incomparably blue sky, swallows in pairs fly away, uttering shrill cries. It is a long way from certain churches to the cathedral ; at a turn in the street we come upon a brotherhood that has halted. The penitents are accosted by their wives and little girls come to see their friends' babies who occupy a prominent place in the procession. In the Calle de las Sierpes, children hold out their hands to the *nazarenos* who, with unflagging patience, let the coveted drop of wax fall into their palms.

From a nearby point, another procession arrives, to the sound of trumpets, guided by Roman soldiers, wearing suits of armour and proudly flourishing standards of an old-fashioned type.

Elsewhere, hurrahs burst forth ; it is the famous "Cristo del Gran Poder" coming from his church, San Lorenzo, which issues forth at Campana. During the nocturnal processions, the emotions and excitement reach a climax. The Virgin of Triana advances along the river amidst the lights — the return of any *Dolorosa* assumes an enchanted aspect at twilight. The crowd merges into an indistinct but enthusiastic mass. The air becomes extremely cool, *saetas* burst from the balconies as though they were the supreme utterance of night and sky ; the *costaleros* toil as they try to go through the too-narrow doorway, and the *capataz* heaps orders and encouraging words upon them ; finally the Virgin's *paso* enters amidst applause and we have the impression of seeing a Basilissa returning to Byzantium after a long absence.

Inside the cathedral the Penitents advance and bow down before the *altar mayor ;* in its turn the *paso* arrives in front of the altar and becomes a living figure : it turns and prepares to bend down ; then, after this moment full of grandeur, it withdraws.

How could men salute the Lord more suitably than by presenting to Him His own portrait or that of His Mother ?

HOLY WEEK IN SEVILLE.
THE BLACK PENITENTS OF THE CHRIST OF THE "GRAN PODER".

HOLY WEEK IN SEVILLE. THE MACARENA ENTERING THE CHURCH OF SAN GIL.

Does the Guadalquivir, as it flows oceanwards amidst the *marismas* or in its various branches, still remember the navigators who discovered and colonized the Americas and the traders whose laden ships used to sail up the river ? Let us imagine the procession on these waters with their rich reflections ; the eager dreams of the discoverers as they sailed off, the gold of the cargoes shipped from America. Did not Sanlucar de Barrameda, near Jerez de la Frontera, witness one of Columbus' departures as well as that of Magellan ?

The memory of those glorious and prosperous centuries can be found westwards, beyond the long incurved coast stretching from the mouth of the Guadalquivir to the region of Huelva. The city, in the heart of a mining district, is lacking in interest but through the nearby ports passed sailors and conquerors. It was at the Monastery of La Rabida, which towers above the junction of the Odiel and the Rio Tinto, amidst its shady trees, that Christopher Columbus found help and encouragement. He sailed on his first voyage from Palos on August 3rd, 1492 ; he landed there the next year, as Cortez, the Conqueror of Mexico, was to do in 1528. Not far from there, Moguer saw just as many ships of those men, greedy for adventure and wealth, who :

> *watched new stars rising*
> *from the depths of the ocean*
> *into an unknown sky.*

So was not the Atlantic but the advanced post of Andalusia for centuries ? Everything there was centred round the sea and from Estremadura, land of the conquerors, to Seville, the gateway to the Indies, the Sierra Morena was but a slowly rising stairway leading to glory and gold.

Today it is on its very soil that we must seek adventure. For the foreigner it is but two steps away : the discovery of a fascinating pilgrimage, that of our Lady of the *Rocio* — the *Blanca Paloma*, the White Dove.

The holy image, which was hidden during the Moslem Invasion in a tree-trunk, near Almonte, not far from the *marismas*, appeared to a hunter, who took it away to put it back in the church of Almonte. The hunter fell asleep and when he awoke, found the statue nowhere ; it had returned to its tree-trunk. In this way the Virgin's desire to be venerated was shown. A pilgrimage was started. Brotherhoods were organized in the neighbourhood. A few days before the feast, they start off in artistically decorated carts. The first one is reserved for the Virgin's standard or *Sinpecado*, of each of them ; the others follow in picturesque procession, while horsemen in Andalusian dress ride along the file of pilgrims. The journey is accomplished amidst songs and the sound of musical instruments. On their arrival, the brotherhoods file past the holy image and the standards are laid at its feet, while the horsemen and pilgrims, animals and people

SEVILLE. THE GUADALQUIVIR AND THE TOWER OF GOLD.

SEVILLE. THE CASA DE PILATOS. THE PATIO.

kneel down. In the evening there is a ball and songs burst forth lauding the miracles of the *Blanca Paloma*.

The next day, the statue itself goes out, carried above the madly excited crowd. Marvellously handsome couples pass us on their steeds; the faithful quarrel over the privilege of carrying the holy image.

Our trip through Andalusia comes to an end on the fantastic note of the spectacle furnished by the pilgrims of the *Rocio*. It was all dreams and sunlight, mystery and picturesqueness, the allurement of a far-away princess.

SEVILLE. DETAIL OF THE AYUNTAMIENTO.

CIUDAD-RODRIGO : THE PALACE OF LOS ALTARES.

A HERD IN ESTREMADURA.

UNIVERSITY OF SALAMANCA.
DETAIL OF THE STAIRCASE.

CHAPTER VI

ESTREMADURA
AND LEON

ESTREMADURA is poor, at least apparently, for, almost as much as Castilla, it is the land where we feel the vital spirit, which provided inspiration for architects and painters, and a desire to conquer in those who discovered America. Pizarro, Morales and Zurbaran were born here; and among the many vast sweeps of tableland in the peninsula, we find here those that are perhaps the most arresting as they stretch towards the nearby mountains beneath the hot sun. Here too, we find an abundance of towns (the word city would not be suitable, because it is too suggestive of our present-day urban centres); they are small or medium-sized. Former-

MERIDA. ROMAN RUINS.

MERIDA. THE ROMAN THEATRE.

CACERES. WOMAN SELLING CANTAROS.

ly they enjoyed sovereign authority and still have a haughty air ; day after day they are bathed in the most authentic atmosphere ; the Mediterranean sky — though the Atlantic is so near, just beyond the strip of territory of Portugal — sheds a profusion of incredibly limpid light and the outlines stand out so distinctly that the countryside seems to have always had the clear-cut contours of the robes of Zurbaran's monks.

In many regions Leon has kept its costumes, songs and traditions. Its landscapes vary between smiling coast and barren sierras. The red soil stretches as far as the houses of Salamanca in gentle undulations ; but in the nearby countryside stock-raising is carried on extensively. In the province of Zamora, the gentle banks of the Rio Esla contrast with the dark, stony valleys of the Sierra de la Culebra. Among the Maragatos, in the land of Leon, we have the impression that a divine curse has doomed the soil to be but rubble and to bring forth only poverty. Yet it is from here that the Reconquest sprang -- from Castile and Leon together.

From Seville to Merida, the railway makes a rather long loop towards Los Rosales and Fuente del Arco to the east, and passes through scenery that the road, which is more direct, will not allow us to admire. But the landscape has so little variety, at least in Andalusia, that it becomes slightly monotonous. At first the train runs along the valley of the Guadalquivir for some hours ; the same olive groves on the low hillsides speckle the same ochreous soil beneath the uniform blue of the sky. Then the track crosses the river, the Andalusian character of the buildings and sites disappears with difficulty ; without a change of the elements composing it, the landscape takes on a new breadth of contour and the vast sweep that makes the countryside of Estremadura so unforgettably soothing to the eye. By way of the Puerto de Llerena, Zafra, Los Santos, Almendralejos, we reach Merida. This district, which was the *Velonia* of the Romans, has an abundance of ruins of that period : Los Santos and Zafra, ancient Roman towns, prepare us for the marvels of Merida. At sunset, in autumn, the countryside blazes with an inimitable symphony of colours. On the huge tablelands, seldom limited by nearby mountains, the soil is tawny and seemingly iridescent with golden grasses. Over the reddish earth creeps the vine, spangled with rust-colour. Ash-grey olive-trees add a rather sad tint to the dull tones and the evening calm floods the whole landscape before night falls. However, to the west the mountain ranges stand out deep black against the orange sky.

The *Augusta Emerita* of the Romans, now modern Merida, has of course attracted archaeologists who excavated and uncovered its ruins. What magnificent themes could a Chateaubriand or, at least, a Barrès find, not only in the ruins the mutilated majesty of which forms such a contrast with the insignificance of the modern town, but also in the very vicissitudes of their history ? Merida would only inspire distaste and melancholy in the visitor who failed to remember that it is human to draw upon old build-

CACERES. ARAB BATHS IN THE CASA DE LAS VELETAS (MUNICIPAL MUSEUM).

ings as the most accessible quarries or else, in changing their purpose, to disfigure them in the pattern of a later civilization. We must shake off our first, unfavourable, impression, and stop to think : of the soil raised by time ; of the theatre, amphitheatre and circus which have been buried ; of the bridge over the Guadiana which was repaired because it was useful ; and finally of the modern town, half-raised from a torpor which still endures, using for its daily life the stones from the temples which might exist, but ignoring the ruins more or less hidden by the soil, and heedless of the useless aqueducts, abandoned to the irremediable wear and tear of time. Once we get over this impression of remoteness we must first rediscover the splendours of the Roman town : it is in the buildings which have been cleared of debris, or preserved ; in the most evocative ruins that we shall capture it ; at the bridge over the Guadiana, above all in the theatre, the circus and the aqueduct of Los Milagros. Once our eyes have taken in all this splendour, we shall be able to reconstitute for ourselves, in the museum, the atmosphere which reimbues with life the artificially arranged evidence of a by-gone world. We shall end our visit at the Arch of Santiago (it is that of Trajan, exorcized under the apostle's name), at the remains of the temples, and at the Alcazaba. They reveal to us a very human and consequently far more natural mixture of the successive periods ; while, from where we stand at the foot of the fortress, a mere glance at the big bridge nearby will remind us that Merida owes its splendour to Rome alone.

To visit the theatre and amphitheatre, we almost leave the city ; their isolated position ensures the silence we like to find in ruins. The theatre, by far the more interesting of the two buildings, was built by Agrippa in 18 B. C. for the recently founded colony of veterans ; but, after a fire, the stage was rebuilt by Trajan and Hadrian, doubtless with the help of Greek artists, judging by the signatures. Not very long ago, only *las siete sillas* were visible, that is to say part of the cavea which assumed the arrangement of seven seats, since it was broken into seven huge blocks at its top ; here, according to legend, the seven Moorish kings who decided the fate of Merida are supposed to have sat. Under Charles III, while the rest of the theatre was still buried, a wall turned these famous seats into a *plaza de toros*. Today the tiers — to arrange them the Romans had utilized the slope of the hill, a habit of theirs — have been cleared, and the stage restored ; it is one of the finest theatres one can see, vast and well balanced, monumental and adorned with statues.

None of the three aqueducts that brought water to the city has been as well preserved or offers such a majestic aspect as that of Segovia. Time has ruined the archways of that of San Lazaro which stands out against the sky. The most impressive, the most poetical is that of Los Milagros ; its ruins frame the landscape in a gigantic trellis. The water of the third one flowed into the conduit in the Roman wall whose foundations still exist along the Guadiana and were used by the Moors in building the Alcazába. As we walk up Santa Eulalia Street we find the chapel dedicated to the saint; the porch was built with stones taken from the Temple of Mars; in the seventeenth century, the ancient inscription : " MARTI. SACRVM VETTILLA. PACVLI " was cancelled by the following one : " No longer to Mars but to Jesus and to his servant Eulalia..." On the acropolis of the Roman city stands the Temple of Diana; the elegance of the columns on the west side remind us of the way the admirable temple of Evora in Portugal soars skywards, so slender and white against the blue. Here it is far less a question of a vision of art than of a purely human lesson : the palace set up in the sixteenth century in the ancient building catches this past glory at the base like a captive bird. The visitor, on leaving the city, will remember not only the resuscitated ruins but also the ancient buildings annexed by men. Here the splendour and gravity of Rome attain such a degree that even though it be dead, it can still offer a few remains to the vicissitudes of the ages. Just as the bridge over the Guadiana, restored by the Visigoths, Philip II and in the nineteenth century, remains the Roman bridge, Merida the drowsy, is the city of Agrippa, the capital of Lusitania, whose name conjures up two pictures, one of rediscovered beauty, the other of captive elegance : a theatre that has risen again, and a temple burdened with a palace.

On leaving Merida we do not head for Badajoz, disappointing and rich in its memories of battles rather than in its works of art, but for Caceres lying northwards. Fortified by the Romans, captured by the Arabs, finally reconquered by Alfonso IX in 1229, it played its part in the most heroic enterprises of Spain : the birth of the Order of Santiago, the Capture of Granada, the conquest of the Americas by those very nobles whose palaces, erected at the end of the fifteenth century and during the sixteenth remain the monumental, warlike ornament of the city. It is the continual coming and going of knights on their way to Seville or going to sea, and of the gold they brought back to build the *casas solariegas*. The stones relate the exciting adventures of the struggle against the Moors, and of journeys to the land of Indians, and time has left on the façades a patina that become daily more golden in the sunlight of Estremadura.

We reach San Juan's church, in the Gothic style and adorned with baroque retables and just beyond it, we walk along alleys towards the enceinte. We enter the old town by way of the Arco and the Torre del Postigo which date back to the Roman period. Henceforth we stroll through the city : narrow streets barred with shadows that are almost too distinct in the light, the transparency of the air, big freestones so immutable that they seem sure of the everlasting nature of the palaces and coats of arms they bear — and a blue grey tonality which sings in the streets; sometimes as we come upon alleys with more humble houses, lime-washed if the sun does not reach them, a chapel or a noble house suddenly looms before us, scarcely troubled by a donkey as it ambles by, laden with milk or vegetables.

TRUJILLO. THE CASTILI O.

Suddenly the light widens out as we come to Santa Ana Square : the beauty of the palace of Los Ovando-Mogollon comes from the regularity of its high windows, the black network of the iron gate and the decoration of massive bossage on the main entrance. At the end of Santa Ana Street, straight and austere between its smooth façades, the Casa de los Golfines de Arriba (that is to say, in the upper part for there is an even finer one in the lower part of the city) leads us into one of the most striking architectural groups in Caceres, set around San Mateo's church. The gravity of the latter, built in the late Gothic style, is brightened by a charming Renaissance portal, a sort of portico with two slender columns, adorned with medallions and surmounted with statues ; the small belfry on the right, poetry incarnate : slender and as if sharpened it stands out against the sky and houses quantities of birds' nests whose occupants soar upwards, with white wings outlined against the heavens. They alight on the Torre de las Cigüenas or the neighbouring palace, the long regular lines and arched windows of which have a noble, almost Florentine strength. The Casa de las Veletas, today a museum, built on the site of the Moorish Alcazar, still has the latter's cistern whose waters, glaucous in the shadows, repeat the arches and columns as in a sad dream. The nearby alley of San Pablo's chapel is slightly curved as it disappears between its white walls defiled by age ; a few steps farther on, we turn around and look up ; in a strip of sky, the melancholy grey trench of the street is crossed by big tufts of plants, higher up rises the little tower of San Mateo whence the eternal white birds soar skywards. At the foot of the Cuesta de la Compania, beyond the baroque chapel and the buildings of the Fathers of the Precious Blood, majestically situated on an embanked terrace whence the whole horizon can be seen, we find the Casa de los Golfines de Abajo ; *plateresco* at the top, widening the frames of its windows from top to bottom, it was built by Sancho Paredes Golfin, chamberlain to Isabella the Catholic. She and Ferdinand dwelt there when Caceres was full of the clash of arms, the echoes of adventure and the tumult of the court : the monogram "Fer de Fer" is that of Fernando, son of the builder, who served Don Fernando, the brother of Charles V.

The nearby church of Santa Maria la Mayor, finished in the middle of the sixteenth century, lies on a square of semi-circular shape whose irregular layout is completed by palaces ; it is not skywards that we must look, as around San Mateo's ; the space is snugly enclosed in a hollow and only evokes the appeased memory of a glorious but irremediably dead past.

However we must continue down, and by way of steeper and more populous streets we reach the church of Santiago, famous for the Christ of Los Milagros, the relics of the Order of Santiago and the reredos for which Alonso Berruguete signed a contract in 1537 but which he never finished. Then we go back up along the enceinte by way of the Aldarve and we admire at random the emblazoned palaces which loom before us here and there in the street itself or at the other end of a short vista — for instance the palace of Juan Cano de Saavedra who married one of the Montezuma daughters. But now we should appreciate the mystery of the streets rather than visit other historic buildings : the long grey and white corridor of the Aldarve with its tall grass playing on the coats of arms and invading the houses, the Arco de la Estrella, its niche and nearby archways ; but it is from a peak near the city, from the sanctuary of the Virgen de la Montaña, that Caceres reveals itself completely : in the sweep of the landscape, sovereign of Estremadura, it stretches luminously beneath an unforgettable sky, embattled, like a holy Amazon, with its palaces, churches and towers.

Our excursions eastwards take us to Trujillo along the roads to Yuste and Guadalupe. At least two aspects of Trujillo can vie with our majestic visions of Caceres : the Plaza Mayor, adorned with an equestrian statue of Pizarro who was born there, but whose beauty comes especially from the palace of his descendants and from that of San Carlos ; its impression of space seems to respond to the dashing advance of the horseman ; the ruined section, which lies at the top of a street surmounted by archways, groups a city of abandoned *casas solariegas* around Santa Maria la Mayor. Among them is the house where Pizarro was born which is now but a mere portal ; grass grows behind the house fronts, but everything is beautiful in this light and with what may be the most moving landscape in the province to gaze upon : an illumination whose memory pursues us like that of a perfection impossible to grasp ; the line of mountains on the horizon, and between them and the city, the flat, fair sweeps of land whose serenity makes the song of cicadas sound melodious, then the nearby castle, all denote an unalterable nobility.

Yuste, the humble convent to which Charles V withdrew and died in 1557, devastated by the Napoleonic wars, has been restored as far as possible ; it still possesses something unique : it affords us the sight of the setting sun on the same horizon — the sun which repeated the approach of his death to the Emperor — and his eyes would recognize the landscape which revealed eternity to him.

It is in the Castellan of Fray José de Sigüenza that the history of Guadalupe should be read. Some priests from Seville fled from the Moorish invasion and hid, in the mountains around the present monastery, the painting of the Virgin that St. Gregory the Great sent to St. Leander — the very one that popular belief attributed to the hand of Luke the Evangelist. Time passed ; shortly before 1329, the painting appeared to a shepherd who was chasing a cow, the cult of the painting increased, the already ancient hermitage grew ; Alfonso XI patronized it, above all after the victory of Salado (1340), the convent became a priory of Hieronymites in 1389 and was entrusted to a great monk and builder, Father Fernando Yañez de Figueroa. In the fifteenth century the main additions were made. The plan adopted is the traditional Benedictine plan ; the church, facing east,

GUADALUPE. GENERAL VIEW.

GUADALUPE. FOUNTAIN IN THE MOZARABIC CLOISTER.

opens southwards on the chapel of Santa Ana, northwards on the great cloister surrounded by the conventual rooms ; farther northwards stands the cloister of the Botica or Pharmacy. The monks were then at one and the same time architects, decorators, goldsmiths, miniaturists and embroiderers ; the collection of choir books, miniatures, embroideries and objects of art of the monastery still bear witness to this. In their life, the marvellous was mingled with holiness ; in the accounts which recall it and which Zurburan was to portray, it seems partly legendary and genuinely radiant. Then came the era of great discoveries, and soon the sixteenth century : Christopher Columbus christened Guadeloupe with the name of the famous Virgin. The conquerors invoked it and the founders of the Escurial set out from her monastery. In the seventeenth century the *capilla mayor* was decorated and the gem of the convent, the sacristy, was built and laid out east of Santa Ana's chapel. Then — despite the *camarin* and canvases by Lucas Giordan dating from the end of the century, despite the eighteenth-century Churrigueresque stalls — the period of torpor began. Portugal, by recovering its independence restored Estremadura to its destiny as a frontier province ; years went by and with them different perils ; today the monastery is exactly the same, to our great delight.

The church belongs to the same line as so many religious edifices in the peninsular and we admire them more than we like them : medieval architecture, baroque decoration, Renaissance gates. We are far more moved by the cloister of the Botica, dating from the beginning of the sixteenth century or at the sight of the central temple (1405) of the great cloister. Their bricks imitate the lines of Gothic buildings made of stone ; but it is the great cloister itself, built in the Mozarabic style by Prior Yañez, which affords us the most subtle delight. Here brick and plaster, the very essence of Almohade art adapt themselves to the requirements of religious life, and the galleries, already cool with a century-old peace, re-echo with the thousand sounds of the garden blooming in their centre : the breeze in the trees, a falling leaf, the continual chirping of birds. Such is the place where the medieval monks used to walk — the monks whose daily and miraculous life was understood and depicted by Zurbaran. To adorn his new sacristy and the adjoining chapel of St. Jerome, Prior Ambrosio de Castelar did not call in an artist who was an expert in baroque devices but he appealed to the painter of spiritual contemplation, already famous for his portraits of the Carthusian monastery of Jerez. Of all the canvases painted by him at Guadalupe in 1638 and 1639, during the sojurns he made there like so many itinerant artists who put up at monasteries, not all are masterly but we can remain indifferent to none. Zurbaran reveals himself to be awkward in depicting horror and conventional in representing the great men of the world, but he is unrivalled when portraying the tranquil, primitive faith of the brothers who had remained true peasants of Estremadura, with big heads and robust hands, in their monkish garb. A few

of these faces never leave the paradise where each of us places the works
of art that have moved him forever : Father Cabañuelas, honoured by a
miracle during his Mass, bowed down by ecstasy as much as by age ; the
ethereal Christ walking before Salmeron's father, and, more touching
than St. Jerome's apotheosis (it is Zurbaran's famous masterpiece), the
temptations embodied by a group of calm, pure, noble musicians who look
more like angels before the descent into hell than companions of Lucifer.

We still have to fathom the beauty of the country, for all Guadalupe —
village and sanctuary — is refreshment for the soul ; vast, flawless sky,
fawn-coloured mountains, olive-trees climbing the gentle slopes, the serene
harshness of the air and countryside, the *pueblo* with its roofs kept low
beneath the monastery but with its balconies overflowing with bright
flowers — and the monastery itself, a peak of hewn stone, an iron diadem
on the height.

From Caceres we should also go to Alcantara whose Roman bridge
and the convent of the Order bearing its name sing its glory — or Coria,
as astonishing as a soldier forsaken by war but still under arms. But Plasencia,
abandoned, would be an eternal regret : the grouping of the two cathedrals
— that of the fourteenth century partly demolished and the new one
unfinished — dominates the terrace where they are perched, and behind
the Renaissance portal whose superimposed storeys outdo one another
in charm, we shall discover the two rivals entangled like monstrous animals
struggling together. Then our road will take us to Salamanca in Leon
and there we shall contemplate one of the most noble landscapes in Spain,
more serene than picturesque, more sweeping than imposing. The mountain
ranges rise in tiers of different heights and depths and in the distance
their dark colour encircles the neighbouring hills covered with olive-trees.
But Salamanca draws near, and the stone becomes fawn, the earth ochreous :
the same shades that give the houses of the city their warm colouring
that is almost a musical resonance. Thus the bewitching city spreads far
and wide the charm which, Cervantes has already said, brings back to it
those who have once enjoyed the delight of living there.

On the right bank of the Rio Tormès spanned by the Roman bridge
and the *puente nuevo*, stands the city — it is the only general view we can
have of it. It looks like a Rome in miniature, powerful and slender, tawny
and imposing ; less luminous with sunlight than with century-old joy.
We first see humble houses scaling the slopes, then, without there being
any proportion between them, up there on a base which we imagine to
be immense, the belfries, cloisters, domes and naves open out ; the two
cathedrals, both of them complete, form a majestic, elaborate mass rendered ethereal by their *cimborios* which seem to float in the air, and by the
huge tower which soars skywards ; the Clericia, i.e., the Jesuits' church,
stands back, surrounded by buildings, like a great bird at rest, feeling the
clouds with its twin towers, and winged tall side galleries ; finally San

225

SALAMANCA. THE ROMAN BRIDGE AND THE CATHEDRAL.

Esteban, the Dominicans' church, whose porch from afar frames in a perfect arch the shadows which seem infinite. And the most beautiful thing in the city is perhaps the elusive quality of the air which is already present. The true Salamanca is not the chiselling of *plateresco* copings but the fringe of light that plays on them. It is not the ornate dizziness of baroque retables but the golden resplendence of their memory. It is not the hubbub of the Plaza Mayor but the rustling of a festive hive hidden there. It is not the ochre colour of the houses but the musical confidences that the stones murmur to those who love their hues. It is not the shadow of a past University but the spirit of the Renaissance that conceived and carried out the façades and the glory and the sun that have given them a patina, as stirring as a face, impervious to decay. Rather than seating its edifices on the hill, the city seems to cling completely with its towers and domes to the stars invisible in daylight, for the town is the waking dream of a Spain poised between the intellect and the heart, delicate, melodious, radiant ; such that, to the Spaniards themselves, it embodies the smile of their soul but never reveals the name of its mystery.

We cross the Roman bridge, a high span over yellowish waters, and towards the right we go up to San Esteban. On its site there used to be a Dominican convent of which there still remains, inside the present cloister, another one dating from the end of the fifteenth century. The church we see, the adjoining gallery, and nearby cloister were built from 1525 on, under the direction of the great architect, Juan de Alava. The open space is immense, the lines clear-cut under the gentle sky, and our eyes contemplate the Convento de la Dueñas (which has an admirable patio) or, in the distance, the little Romanesque church of St Thomas-of-Canterbury, rustic and low-roofed, or, even further away, the college of Calatrava, a true eighteenth-century palace ; but they always come back to this façade, to its monumental arch — it seems as if the impalpable air, impregnated with serene beauty, continues to pass across the delicate sculpture and to caress the fair shapes — with its light and noble archways. Inside, the *coro alto* above the entrance is decorated with a *Triumph of the Blessed Sacrament* by Palomino, the naive, delectable historian of artists and a painter himself ; our eyes are drawn towards the retable of the *altar mayor* (1693) for which José Churriguera — the family of this name lavished its talent on seventeenth and eighteenth-century baroque Salamanca — imagined a monumental structure with spiral columns ; if it is not lacking in a sense of grandeur, it is however surprising to find such a work in this church with its pure lines, where it seems the very negation of religious peace. But in the city everything becomes harmony, one has but to push back a door and we find monacal fervour in the cloister. In that of the old convent, the enclosure makes the silence intense and the galleries are given over to memories. In the old monastery, a centre of scientific knowledge, Christopher Colombus sought help and advice, and this evocation brings back beneath the vaults the glorious plans which gave birth to an epic.

Let us turn our back on San Esteban[1]. At some distance before us looms the New Cathedral, almost contemporaneous with the Dominican church and the University buildings. So rich was the city at that period and so outstanding its artists. Begun in 1513 by Juan Gil de Hontañon, continued by his son Rodrigo who also built the Monterrey Palace and carried on during two centuries in the Gothic style originally adopted, it hides the Old Cathedral as a gigantic hull protects a smaller ship from the fury of the elements. As we advance, the mass seems to be stressed more by the aisle chapels on the ground and by the gables, above, as well as by the tower ; the sculpture in the portals is set beneath flamboyant arches and the charm of the main façade clashes with the mighty eighteenth-century corner tower which was consolidated after the Lisbon earthquake. Inside, the chapter, already penniless after building the edifice, was only able to construct the *silleria*, the outer part of the *coro* and the gate done by the Frenchman, Dupérier. The resulting bareness, so unusual in Spain and Spanish sanctuaries makes the ethereal lines even more perceptible and we admire the grace and the radiant light from the *cimborio*, a bowl of light hanging over our heads. The secondary chapels contain works of art which are also moving souvenirs : the twelfth-century copper and enamel statue of the *Virgen de la Vega* the *Cristo de las Batallas* which was that of the Cid and the *Piedad* in which the sculptor Carmona adapted his memories of Michelangelo to his temperament. A few steps take us to the Old Cathedral, situated on a lower level, and appreciably reduced on the side near the new one. In this plain, spacious but discreet architecture, after the ostentation of its neighbour's vaults, early Gothic mingles with Romanesque architecture ; above the statues of angels of the Apocalypse calling for the Judgment, the *torre del gallo* opens its luminous dome, waiting for centuries to welcome the divine arrival. This theme has been totally carried out in the painting on the semi-dome of the *capilla mayor ;* while angels in flight sound trumpets, Christ separates the chosen from the damned. Behind the altar, in the small compartments of the retable, the life of Christ and of the Virgin unfolds, painted by Nicolàs Florentino in the middle of the fifteenth century — and with his brush Italian charm invades the light, empty church. Splendid chapels open into the cloister ; behind a sumptuous gate, one contains the alabaster tomb of Don Diego de Anaya, another is covered by a Mozarabic vault, a third recalls the trials of the doctors of yore : they merged triumphant to the ringing of bells or were ejected through the *puerta de los carros*. Such is the visit to the Old Cathedral which seems to be a forbidden domain, for the new one, and the cloister,

---

(1) Not far from there is also the picturesque " Torre del Clavero ", the remains of a fourteenth-century baronial hall.

SALAMANCA. THE "CATEDRAL VIEJA".

SALAMANCA. THE CASA DE LAS CONCHAS. DETAIL OF THE FAÇADE.

hide it from the street and only the *cimborio* appears, strange and pure, covered with scales and distinct against the sky.

Then Salamanca has been seen in its majestic aspect. At the Patio

SALAMANCA. THE PLAZA MAYOR.

SALAMANCA. THE DOORWAY OF THE UNIVERSITY.

de las Esculas, it unites in a minimum space, on two sides of a quiet square, the most elegant settings of its art. In spite of the unfortunate statue of Fray Luis de Léon whose fame deserved something better than this mediocre effigy, opposite commonplace houses that are so modest near their admirable neighbours, we see but the three marvels of the Renaissance : the door of the Hospital del Estudio, the door (quite similar to but smaller than that of the University) and the Patio de las Escuelas Menores ; the façade of the University itself which is adorned over the entrance with medallions of the Catholic Sovereigns and Charles V between compartments of stone point-lace, is one of the summits of *plateresco* art, delicate without ceasing to be robust, graceful in its detail while remaining monumental. We have the impression that these doors no longer open on anything, but that they close the shrine where all the memories of intellectual Salamanca vibrate in the golden air. Then the alleys and inns swarmed with life, the sons of wealthy families congested the pavement with their sumptuous retinues ; here Olivarès took form ; at the Roman bridge, Lazarillo di Tormès, a *picaro* among so many others, began his adventurous career ; and the half-starved student sought out among the young nobles the future archbishop or minister. It often happened that once the latter were in power they remembered their fellow-students at Salamanca. But the beauty of the shrine today prevails over the evocation of an existence for which it was only the magnificent dwelling. It used to shelter knowledge ; the life of yore, disappearing, abandoned it to its solitude and our contemplation, and it has actually become knowledge itself. Indeed the human hand only required a distance of a few yards and the thickness of a wall to erect on three occasions the most triumphal and elegant doors through which passed, day by day, all those — scholars, students and professors — who by making the mind their profession honoured mankind even more.

To be nearer the University and to dominate it, the Jesuits wanted to settle in the heart of the city. They had to overcome tenacious opposition but they triumphed and the rivalry of their college helped to bring down its rival. Near the Renaissance façades as thin as a stage set, the mass of their seventeenth-century buildings, spacious but dominating looms into a gigantic rectangle. The patio is one of the most majestic of the baroque period ; the retables of the church, which grow lighter as we approach the *altar mayor*, blaze with gilding ; the skyward soar of the façade becomes lines fleeing into the blue firmament when we contemplate the towers and the high-relief representing the Assumption from the patio of the neighbouring house : the Casa de la Conchas, whose façade is adorned with shells (hence its name) and which is one of the most noble civil buildings dating from the days of the Catholic Sovereigns. Beyond it, the Romanesque church of San Benito seems coiled up, so to speak, in the little provincial square, then the Monterrey Palace, which was never finished but is so beautiful that it makes us forget its insipid imitations, and, opposite, the

233

CIUDAD-RODRIGO. HENRY II CASTLE.

BETWEEN SALAMANCA AND ZAMORA.

Convento de Agustinas, enriched by an *Immaculate Conception* by Ribera. It is very firm, as we might expect it to be from this powerful painter, but strangely tender if we compare it with so many examples of *St. Bartholomew delivered to his Flayers*. The college of the Irish, where Philip II housed the seminarists of that nation, has one of the most harmonious Renaissance patios and from its terrace, as from the nearby Paseo San Francisco, the city below spreads in all its splendour. But a chapel attracts us : the Capilla de la Vera Cruz, whose decoration inside evokes Mexican baroque and this word alone calls to mind the development in a far country of an art that produced so many masterpieces in Salamanca.

But let us wander here and there, and without seeking it we shall come upon the last marvel : the Plaza Mayor. Built in the reign of Philip V it is better than a place or date in architecture — it is a perfect poem punctuated by its four closed façades, noble in aspect but enlivened by details. It is here that Salamanca lives and we have not seen or felt anything of the city if during the day we have not munched a delicacy (a *yema*, some *huevos de santo*, or *mazapanes*) in a sweet-shop, sampled *gambas* in a café, or paraded interminably in the lines of young men or young girls who are carefully separated and only meet when they cross from opposite directions. The babble of their remarks, the hubbub of their interjections, and the shuffle of their footsteps form the unforgettable murmur of Salamanca ; spending an hour in the Plaza Mayor, means learning to know the perfect music that the conversation of a crowd can produce in the perfection of its setting. And as the enchantment of the city triumphs over the accuracy of our memories we shall think, like Unamuno, — the last of the great minds to attach his name to that of the city — that here flows a spiritual life more intense than in other cities of greater populations, trade or industry... Salamanca, the song of stones, sky and crowd : wit and charm, oh ! nostalgic memory of the heart !

Not far from this mellow city, St. Teresa died. Alba de Tormès, where she drew her last breath, still keeps part of her body and is now a place of pilgrimage. Ciudad Rodrigo is one of those medium-sized cities with admirable historic buildings and a fascinating atmosphere which, even more than big tourist centres, delight the traveller. A "Parador" has been installed in the castle ; the streets are lined with palaces, and the cathedral, which juxtaposes Romanesque and Gothic, has a flamboyant *silleria* on which the famous Rodrigo Aleman exerted his zest.

But the countryside, with its villages, beauty spots, traditions and customs, of this privileged province will perhaps attract us even more. The region of La Alberca, ranked as a national historic building, leads us to the legendary Valley of Las Batuecas and the miserable district of the Hurdès, Luis Bunuel's "Land without bread". Processions file between the white houses with projecting balconies on the Feast of the Assumption, and for the Pilgrimage of Our Lady of the Pena de Francia on September 8.

236

ZAMORA. THE BANKS OF THE DUERO.

LEON CATHEDRAL. THE MAIN PORCH.

The ancient costumes have survived in all their beauty. The laces form
points on the peasant women's foreheads, from their necks hang countless
strings of beads heavy with crosses, crucifixes, balls and various objects ;
in their ceremonial costumes, hieratic in their straight black garments, the
peasant women are the perfect representation of proud and archaic beauty.
The brightly clad men, in shirt-sleeves, white stockings, waistcoats and tight
breeches, wear capes slung over one shoulder. The serenity of some old

LEON. SAN ISIDORO. FRESCO IN THE VAULT OF THE PANTHEON OF THE KINGS
OF LEON. SAINT LUKE.

A LANDSCAPE IN LEON

men, whose faces are furrowed by age and the hard work in the fields, comes as much from the peace of a kind of life that is centuries-old as from approaching eternity ; they seem to be the mute answer to the commandment: 'Thou shalt live by the sweat of thy brow'.

Zamora has been a dormant city since the Romanesque period when several churches were built and the cathedral begun. The calm air of the countryside which spreads over the opposite bank of the Duero brings serenity : the long, long streets which follow the river interminably, the absence of wide thoroughfares, make up a sad rustic town which seems farther and farther from the present time as we approach the cathedral. This stands at the end of the city and lifts its *cimborio*, covered with scales like that of Salamanca, above an entrance which was rebuilt on the transept side in the classical style. When the traveller emerges from the narrow, endless streets on to the well-proportioned square, he is seized by a sudden emotion ; the space is immense, the lines of the portal noble, and the *cimborio* unexpected.

We continue northwards in the direction of Leon — reluctantly leaving the road which leads to Orense by way of Puebla de Sanabria ; the mountains here are wild and dark, the villages scarce, the passes high, and our trip across the region procures striking impressions.

Leon, the proud city which was the most considerable Christian town in Spain in the tenth century, retains only the glorious buildings of its past. The atmosphere has vanished and the visitor is deceived who hoped to find far more than splendours of art lost amidst the indifference of banal public walks, modern squares and thoroughfares intersecting at right angles. Yet the archaeologist finds one of the richest groups of buildings in the peninsula here. The ancient Romanesque abbey of San Isidoro still has vaults with magnificent twelfth-century paintings, representing scenes from the Apocalypse and the life of Christ, the tombs of the Kings of Leon — and the sarcophagi are lined up in this Saint-Denis that was laid waste by the French invasion. Of all the Spanish cathedrals this one is the most nearly related to our Gothic edifices and especially to Notre-Dame in Rheims. As it appears with its lofty façade, its network of flying buttresses and its sculptured portals, it seems to have come directly from beyond the Pyrenees ; a careful visit brings about faint differences in the first impression but it may be that in a country which hold the picturesque and unexpected in store for us at each moment we are vexed because the edifice offers us its beauty without reserving a surprise ; we should like to be astonished still more. Mostly a thirteenth-century work — Master Henry of Burgos Cathedral worked on it — possessing one of the oldest *sillerias* in Spain, a painted fifteenth-century retable by Nicolas Francès (unfortunately not completely restored), stained-glass windows dating from the thirteenth to the sixteenth centuries, it conquers us little by little. In France we should have been beguiled at once ; here it must persuade us.

241

San Marcos, a spacious edifice which belonged to the Order of Santiago and was built at the beginning of the Renaissance, extends a façade on which *plateresco* art has lavished the most delicate ornaments.

From Leon, we may go to San Miguel de Escalada or Sahagun, with wonderful medieval churches.

Towards Galicia, we cross the region of the Maragatos, barren and wretched. Its capital, Astorga, which looms up dusty and sad, is in its likeness. In the city we suddenly come upon a tall Renaissance façade : it is that of the cathedral, whose beauty blazes forth in the dull streets ; a few yards away the bishop's palace, by the Catalan Gaudi, dumbfounds us once more. Contrasts usual in Spain ? It is rather nature dominated by a race which, trapped in a desert, instead of fleeing, made beauty spring forth, and more recently, the fantastic.

ASTORGA CATHEDRAL. WEST DOORWAY : DETAIL OF THE DOOR.

LEQUEITIO. THE QUAYS.

LUGO CATHEDRAL.
CHRIST IN GLORY ON THE SPANDREL.

CHAPTER VII

THE ATLANTIC COAST

SINCE the far-off day when we left Madrid and crossed so many regions of different attractions, we have kept two panels in store for us among the thousand and one pictures in the Prado; for they

243

heralded the ultimate joy that Spain reserved for us — in the heart of Galicia, the visit to Santiago, St. James-of-Compostella.

Just as a painter of the Aragon school could see them at the end of

AUTUMN PLOUGHING IN GALICIA.

ORENSE. BRIDGE OVER THE MINO.

the fifteenth century, one represents the embarkation at Jaffa of the body of St. James; the other, its transference to Galicia.

But these episodes are only two among many others in the evolution of an illustrious and legendary story. St. James, who had come to evangelize Spain, is supposed to have landed at the little port of *Iria Flavia*, now El Padron in Galicia. He is supposed to have preached there for several years and then gone back to the East. After his martyrdom, the body, accompanied by his faithful disciples, was embarked at Jaffa and the ship headed for *Iria Flavia* where it touched land, after a miraculous crossing. The saint's tomb, guarded by his disciples Athanasius and Theodore, later buried with their master, was forgotten and abandoned during the Roman persecutions. In the ninth century, a star appeared — hence *Campus Stellae*, Compostello, the field of the star — and revealed the site of the relics. A new temple was built to house them; around it grew up a town, Santiago de Compostella,

SAINT JAMES-
OF-COMPOSTELLA.

CATHEDRAL OF SAINT JAMES-OF-COMPOSTELLA : DETAIL OF THE PORCH OF GLORY.

SAINT JAMES-OF-COMPOSTELLA.
WOMAN PRAYING AT THE ENTRANCE OF THE CATHEDRAL.

SAINT JAMES-OF-COMPOSTELLA. WEST FAÇADE OF THE CATHEDRAL.

and the pilgrimage became famous. After the apostle appeared to the soldiers fighting the Moors at Clavijo, he was no longer invoked only as the

SAINT JAMES-OF-COMPOSTELLA. HOSPITAL SQUARE.

evangelizer of the peninsula, but as the leader of the reconquest as well. When El Mansour captured and looted the city, the whole of Christendom was appalled.

Cluny, the chief monastery of a powerful order, directed by exceptional Abbots, was instrumental in organizing help for the Christian kingdoms of the north of Spain, also in aiding them in their crusade and in creating many other monasteries beyond the Pyrenees; the bishops and abbots were chosen from among the black monks of the order. "The ways of St. James" followed by the pilgrims from France, followed several itineraries in that country. In Spain one of them passed through Canfranc and Jaca; they joined at Puente de la Reina. Logrono, Najera, Santo Domingo de Silos, Burgos, Fromista, Sahagun, Leon, Astorga, Ponferrada were the stages on the way to Galicia. In this province itself, the pilgrims were lodged in the huge hostelries of the monasteries such as Sobrado de los Monjes and Osera.

These itineraries, because of their very origin, and the number of Frenchmen who followed them, became channels for French art — with all the gradations which inevitably resulted from the influence of Islamic and Mozarabic art, above all in sculpture. One type of church is to be found along these roads, naturally with various interpretations, but answering the common purpose of receiving crowds. Inside a spacious edifice, the plan comprises a choir surrounded by an ambulatory and radiating chapels to facilitate the circulation of the pilgrims. The point of departure was doubtless the destroyed church of the Apostle to the Gauls, St. Martin of Tours; the perfect type is St. Sernin in Toulouse, the most moving example in a wild setting is St. Foy of Conques. In Spain we find Santiago Cathedral and its admirable Porch of Glory, by Master Matthew, one of the high points of Romanesque art.

So we must adopt the naive and picturesque soul of the fifteenth-century painter and see in all Galicia, cities, historic buildings and country-side, ports and coast, an incomparable whole, illuminated by radiant Santiago, the holy city rich not only in memories of Romanesque but of baroque and Renaissance art also.

The tower and apse of the twelfth-century church of the Caaveiro stand among palm-trees. The Romanesque portal of that of Elvina rises at the top of moss-grown stairs. From the foliage emerge the imposing but harmonious masses of monasteries. Before the tiers of mountains the sanctuary of the Hermits of Viana del Bollo lifts its towers between the tangle of houses, rising by degrees, and a lofty gallery of windows. Beside the baroque church, the frames of the ruined cloisters of Sobrado stretch like giant links amidst perennial plants. Osera, partly rebuilt after a fire in 1572, deserved the name of the Escorial of Galicia. And Samos and Celanova with their peaceful silence among the trees...

Four towns prepare us directly for Santiago : Orense, Ribadavia, Pontevedra, Lugo. The first one offers us the charm of its old quarter.

SANTILLANA DEL MAR. THE COLLEGIATE CHURCH.

In the streets with their wide paving-stones, everything seems grey, not a sad grey but a poetical hue. Is not the quiet little square near the Cathedral an oration in stone, preceding the visit to the church ? The latter shows us an imitation of the Porch of Glory ; it still has part of its polychromy. Inside we admire the Renaissance dome, and, among other works of art, the retable of the *altar mayor* with the multiple flamboyant arcading of its canopies above the life of Christ, and the fragments of another retable of champlevé enamel which bears witness to the wide-spread influence of the work of Limoges.

In Ribadavia, whose verdant site dominates the junction of the Miño and the Avia, picturesque sights abound at the ends of the streets, edged with arcades or plunging down in steps ; views of churches, palaces, the ruins of the castle and the smiling majestic countryside. In a setting of vertical embankments and tall trees rise the Chapel of the Virgen del Portal and the apse of Santo Domingo.

At Pontevedra, we shall remember the harmonious, monumental sixteenth-century façade of Santa Maria la Mayor and the museum. At Lugo, near the ruins of the enceinte, the cathedral, despite its splendid yet rather cold seventeenth-century facade, is Romanesque, like that of Santiago and still has a period spandrel.

Nature itself has made the region of St. James a privileged one. The shore, deeply indented not only by the sinuous line of the coast but also by the deep gorges of the *rias*, is a mixture of green foliage and sheets of blue water beneath a sky that is often grey but sometimes dazzling. There are many excellent ports : La Coruña, Ferrol, Vigo. The last is uninteresting but the bay, where the gold-laden galleons from America disappeared in 1702, is unforgettable. The calm, almost tender sea, steals inland as gently as a great river, still keeping the deep blue of the ocean. Sections of forests tumble down the mountains ; oaks, chestnut-trees and lemon-trees, orange-trees and laurels, too, grow on this soil dampened by the presence of the ocean. Shall we evoke our Brittany ? The latter is more fundamentally melancholy, less bright, less grandiose. Galicia, despite its frequent rain, would make us think of a country in the flowery and majestic romances of the Round Table, that King Arthur might have placed at the disposal of James the Apostle.

But it is quite different inland. The edge of the Meseta and the coastal mountains, at their junction, produce veritable knots of sierras and we find once again — between Orense and Puebla de Sanabria for instance — wild, proud Spain.

As soon as we arrive in Santiago, the harmony of the colours and the charm of the city lay hold of us. The houses are built of the same grey stone — are they not the reflections of the sky with its scudding clouds ? At once, on our left, when we arrive from Pontevedra, we see gardens ;

254

among the flowers rise the church of Santa Susana and that of Our Lady del Pilar, frail and exquisite with its two turrets, and the College of San Clemente, stretching on both sides of a central door with two tiers of columns. The Paseo de la Herradura affords one an enchanting glimpse of the chief historic buildings, hardly concealed by a fringe of leaves; beyond some little gardens, the back of the palace of Rajoy stands out, so huge that it might be that of a king; above this mass, we see the cathedral towers soaring skywards so affectingly; those of the Obradoiro — the baroque façade which hides the Romanesque church and immediately precedes the Porch of Glory — of the Crown, the Treasure and the Clock; it seems as though the light never tires of imagining new lighting effects, through the airy boughs, for those far away towers.

We soon direct our steps towards the Rua del Villar, dark and lined with arcades, and almost medieval at least in inspiration; and we come to the Plaza de las Platerias in front of one of the portals of the cathedral transept.

The main walls of the edifice, begun about 1078 and probably built by Frenchmen, were finished about 1125. It was only a little later, from 1168 to 1188, that the Porch of Glory was built. The builder, Master Matthew, is made known to us by an inscription on the work itself. After the first golden age of the Romanesque period, each century embellished the admirable church where pilgrims thronged. The end of the seventeenth century and the eighteenth were, thanks to its archbishops, a second golden age.

Today later constructions everywhere hide the original cathedral. Around some perfect churches the centuries, as if to defend them, have hastened their impulse and left the ramparts of their art on the walls. So the baroque age, unfurling its wave here and there, resolves itself into this climax of towers intoxicated with their height and of faces as curved and bent as gigantic flowers.

In only one spot does the Romanesque church see daylight : on the Plaza de las Platerias which, for this single reason, would be unique in the city. The two Romanesque arches of the Puerta de las Platerias open amidst a splendid sculptured decoration which was altered after the north door was destroyed and therefore no longer corresponds to a logical order. But what harmony there is in the general arrangement of the semi-circular arches, the spandrels, the upper tier of sculpture and the second storey of windows ! Among the statues and fragments of groups, dating from the end of the eleventh century or the beginning of the twelfth, some are of an exceptional quality : David the musician, an aristocrat to his finger-tips, whose robe falling over his crossed legs forms folds like the ripples of a river — Adam, just after his creation, whom God is pressing between His out-stretched hands as if to make sure of his existence — the Adulteress on the left spandrel, undressed and desirable despite her death's head — and on the upper tier the Saviour and St. James, with faces of rare integrity.

In the absence of this Puerta the square would be beautiful thanks to its other façades and its atmosphere : the towers and walls unite in the same grey stone symphony. On the left the outer wall of the cloister which was planned by Rodrigo Gil de Hontanon and which is topped by a coping similar to that of Monterrey Palace in Salamanca, is dominated at the

BILBAO. THE PORT.

SAN SEBASTIAN. SEA VIEW FROM MOUNT URGULL.

corner of the Calle de Fonseca by the tower of the Treasure ; behind the
latter looms a stretch of lofty baroque façade, then the plain sweep of wall
which bounds this side of the cloister. On the right, the tower of the clock
built between 1316 and 1680 or thereabouts, is decorated in the baroque
style. The elegant Casa del Cabildo is of the same style. The water of the
Fuente de los Cabollos plays in this noble stone setting.

A flight of steps runs right up through the neighbouring square,
that of the Quintana or Los Literarios, so spacious and severe. The dome
of the cathedral, finished in 1666, and the apse rise above the seventeenth-
century buildings. The long line of the latter stretches out in an unforeseeable
and harmonious rhythm marked by the Clock tower, the corners of the
buildings, the façades of the Puerta Real and the Puerta Santa : the latter
hides the twelfth-century door which is only opened for holy or jubilee
years.

On the other side of the transept the Azabacheria corresponds to the
Puerta de las Platerias. Here rose the so-called Francigena door : before
it flowed the fountain where pilgrims used to purify themselves. In the
present decoration, dating from the second half of the eighteenth century,
neo-classicism prevails over the baroque. Opposite it stretches the immense
façade, finished in 1738, of the Benedictine abbey of San Martin Pinario,
now a seminary. Forming an angle with the cathedral, the new bishop's
palace, also an eighteenth-century work, contains the twelfth-century
palace by Gelmirez ; it is one of the most interesting buildings of Spanish
secular architecture.

Finally, by a vaulted passage-way, we enter the Plaza del Hospital
— oh ! beautiful vision in its serene harmony ! Opposite us Rajoy so classical
and majestic ; on the right, the Hospital Real, founded by the Catholic
Sovereigns in 1499, built according to Enrique de Egas's plans : all of it
is very plain except its *plateresco* door done by some Frenchmen ; on the
left, the Colegio San Jeronimo and its fifteenth-century sculptured portal ;
on the last side, between the bishop's palace and the lofty façade of the
cloister buildings terminated by the Crown tower, rises the Obradoira.
Its façade rises from its perron as from a pedestal. This work, mostly
done by Fernando Casas (1738-1750) soars against the depth of the sky
which it transpierces and peoples with the infinite world of its sculptures
like a forest ready to take wing.

Shall we regret that the Obradoira conceals the Porch of Glory ?
Already we are indebted to it for the sight of this astonishing skyward
flight of forms ; now it overwhelms us with the surprise of a sublime group
and indeed it is the finest protection that the eighteenth century could
have found for the Romanesque marvel ; it seems as though it purposely
embellished itself to honour it in its own way. The medieval Portico of
Glory had chosen the loftiness of the soul and theological inspiration ;
this one, more secular, can only lift a building skywards, but a breath

of grandeur blows between them and, every evening, if the sky is cloudless, the Obradoira becomes the magnificent, skilfully wrought gateway which, by directing the beams of the setting sun on the innumerable statues, filters a rare poetic glory upon them.

Master Matthew's work, which must be placed in the great family of the spandrels of Moissac, Vézelay, Autun, and Conques, owes its originality to the artistic predilection for forms, mass or relief, and to the general movement. The left side is devoted to the Church of the Jews, or Synagogue. The statues of the splayed jambs represent prophets ; in one of the arch mouldings there are the Saviour, Adam and Eve and still more prophets. The great central porch is that of the Church of Christ : on the right, four apostles, on the left, four prophets ; on the door mullion, the tree of Jesse and the statue of St. James ; on the spandrel, Christ the Redeemer amidst the evangelists and angels bearing the instruments of His Passion ; on the archivolt, the Ancients of the Apocalypse. The right-hand door shows us the Church of the Gentiles. The decoration continues on the other side of the present façade of the Obradoiro, showing above all St. John the Baptist and a very beautiful Esther opposite the central arch.

Through the doors, the cathedral appears in the perfection of the vaults (we must leave aside the baroque decoration which is particularly unfortunate in the *capilla mayor*). Nowhere inside the building shall we contemplate such a sight, not even in the crypt where the relics of St. James and his companions, Athanasius and Theodore, are venerated.

The admirable sixteenth-century cloister, built according to Juan de Alava's plans, the many tombs, the Catedral Vieja (the name is wrong for it is merely a crypt under the Porch of Glory, that it supports) afford us the beauties of architecture and sculpture.

And now let us wander through the city, visiting the Renaissance college of Fonseca which opens on to a flower garden and whose patio is made brighter by an even more charming garden ; stopping in front of the Romanesque porch of Santa Maria Salomé, so picturesque in its quaint old street, or entering Santa Maria del Mar, slightly outside the city. The baroque sanctuaries which are particularly enjoyable here because of the hard grey stone will reveal an unknown aspect of this art to us.

We shall evoke, or we shall see, the agitation which takes possession of this city on the feast of the apostle, when the eight *gigantones*, stored away during the year in an annex of the cathedral, carry through the crowd the gigantic image of pilgrims of different origins.

But we are irresistibly attracted to the squares which surround this holiest of churches ; that of the Obradoiro, so flat and serene that it seems to expect at any moment the Last Judgment, that of the Quintana, as sternly plain as a Roman square, and that of Las Platerias whose towers, arches and fountain, in the sunlight, are so merry that they might be Venetian.

ONDARROA.

And perhaps, on a rainy night, along the archways, with the regular gaps of light made by the dim globes, these same walls, these eternal towers, will draw us there for one last look. Oh, cathedral! So hazy in the darkness and drizzle and already nostalgic : are we not sure that in a few hours we shall only be able to love Santiago merely as the memory of a perfect city ?

***

The Asturias, the region of Santander, the Basque provinces and Navarre will afford us the succession of their landscapes and great cities until we reach the French frontier.

In the heart of an industrial region, Oviedo, capital of the Asturias, was laid waste for the first time by a revolutionary movement in 1934 and the second time during the Civil war. The Gothic cathedral, built between the fourteenth and the sixteenth centuries, has a very fine portal with three archways and a single very graceful tower ; it is above all famous for the sculpture and the treasure of its *Camara Santa* which suffered greatly in 1934 and is once again open to the public : the most exquisite work is perhaps the Cross of the Angels ordered by Alfonso the Chaste (808). Very old memories of medieval Spain abound in the surrounding countryside : is not Covadonga, the site of the first victory against the Moslems, about fifty miles from the city ? The mountain and valley have become a national park but the chapel of Santa Maria and the basilica of the Virgen de las Batallas recall the historic memory and the religious meaning of the victory.

After the atmosphere of Santiago, do we want to feel quite out of our element ? If so, let us take the road which leads to Leon. Amidst impressive landscapes, by way of the Pajares pass separating the Asturias from Leon we go through workers' villages with their black houses, near the coal-mines.

The itinerary we follow along the coast shows us the many ports in their more or less spacious bays, before a faraway mountain range. Ribadesella sprawls cosily ; Unquera-Bustio is the starting-point for a visit to the Picos de Europa, the imposing group of which the mountains of Covadonga form only the western part ; San Vicente de la Barquera, dominated by its castle, has fine churches and its site on the heights is very picturesque.

Slightly away from the sea, a few miles before reaching Santander, in the green countryside with its gentle valleys, we discover one of the gems of the Atlantic coast : Santillana del Mar. This big village seems to have been saved up for the end of our trip to remind us of all the little towns which have not only kept one or two ancient buildings but also the unchanged atmosphere of a wondrous past. The capricious streets intersect, edged with *casas solariegas* — the street names and those of the houses all breathe poetry : the Calle de Juan Infante, that of the Cantón, the Casa de los Villas, that of the Marquis of Santillana, the Casa de Busta-mente y de Horo... Somet'mes trees rise above garden walls and the long lines of stern grey façades, adorned with balconies and justifiably proud of their century-old escutcheons, disappear. On a square near fields whence come birds' cries and the distant murmur of the countryside, rises the collegiate church. Tradition has it that in the sixth century, the body of Santa Juliana, or Illana (who is supposed to have given her name to the country), was transfered to it ; a monastery was founded which became the present Romanesque collegiate church. In the galleries of the cloister, the capitals are adorned with rich sculpture.

Near Santillana, the grottoes of Altamira contain prehistoric paintings which are considered one of the finest examples of this art. Bison, horses and various other animals decorate the vaults whose very bulges were used to obtain a finer impression.

Continuing eastwards we reach Santander, a great port and modern city, a seaside resort and the seat of an international summer University. The sojourns of the royal family made Sardinero beach fashionable and its popularity has not abated.

Even farther eastwards, we enter the Basque provinces which are invaded in summer by visitors eager to find a cool spot.

Bilbao, a great industrial centre and modern city with well laid-out avenues, has an old quarter with narrow, tangled-up streets, with a wealth of picturesque sights ; the church of Santiago was a halting-place for pilgrims on their way to St. James-of-Compostella.

San Sebastian is not only the fashionable resort with its admirable beach stretching in front of the Concha and its elegant, almost Parisian districts — it is also the group of old houses huddling together in the shadow of Mount Urgull.

We cannot leave the Basque country without visiting the astonishing baroque monastery built on the site of the house where St. Ignatius Loyola was born ; it is about thirty one miles from San Sebastian. As we gaze upon it, we remember so very many convents with tormented forms and imposing masses that we have discovered along the way.

Fuenterrabia and Irun might be our last halt on our way to Saint-Jean-de-Luz and Biarritz ; but we owe Spain something better than that trite departure ; we shall leave it by visiting Navarra. Pampeluna, in a rugged landscape of coloured mountains, will offer us its steep streets where young bulls dash down, like an avalanche, through the eager crowd, on *Feria* days. The cathedral, containing the tombs of Charles III of Navarre and his wife Eleanor of Castile, is especially interesting for its holy relics and the sculpture of its Gothic cloister which shows French influence.

Estella, a small city where the court of Navarre resided, offers us its Romanesque and Gothic churches in the privileged atmosphere of cities where stone and spirit are intact.

TOLOSA. THE BANKS OF THE ORIA.

PAMPELUNA. IN THE BULL RING AFTER THE "ENCIERRO".

And Roncevalles by means of the memory of Roland, by its vast convent where a Virgin of Toulouse, made of wood and covered with sheets of silver, and dating from the early fourteenth century, is venerated, and also by means of the memory of the pilgrims of Santiago, and the splendour of its mountains, will provide us with the farewell we owe to the peninsula : the glorious history which became an epic, the devotion to the Mother of God and the Apostle James, the unrivalled scenery — precisely all that we have loved during thousands of miles and that we see for the last time.

ALTAMIRA. MAGDALENIAN PAINTING. A HIND.

BARCELONA. IN THE HARBOUR.

FOUNTAIN AT IGLESIAS, NEAR MADRID.

CONCLUSION

"I am he who in his mind's eye surpasses all poets", wrote Cervantès in his confession of the *Journey of Parnassus*. The definition applies just as well to the genius who tried to explain the Spanish soul as to this soul and the country itself. Does not the long series of French travellers and writers, who were too often superficial observers, bear witness to the fact that Spain, in its essential spirit, carries us far beyond reality?

267

Let us limit ourselves to a few contemporary writers who are particularly indebted to the peninsula. Barrès pursued the incarnation of his dreams in Toledo — but who has expressed with such exact elegance the secret, then forgotten, of the incomparable city ? Claudel nonchalantly raises the historic scaffolding on which he unfolds the drama of Prouhèze and Rodrigo — but he understands the baroque tendency of the nation, the giddiness that overcame the great discoverers when they thought of the void of the unknown Indies, that half of the planet still to be evangelized. Montherlant wraps himself up in the inhuman mysticism of a master of Santiago — but he renders the haughty splendour

THE MONASTERY OF SANTO DOMINGO DE SILOS.

TOLEDO. BEHIND THE CATHEDRAL.

with a gesture of his own, he shows us the attraction of death for this race, and going even further, the fascination of nothingness.

All of them, though failing to give a precise picture of Spain, have done homage to its myth which is to it what resplendence is to light.

And to us, who have travelled much too fast, the greatness of the country seems to reside in its unlimited potentiality for inspiring heroism and beauty. Sublime at its apogee, as few nations have ever been, now stripped of one of the biggest empires on earth, it remains astonishingly faithful to itself. Neither the historic buildings, nor the sky, nor the land have changed. And the mere name of Spain has the rare privilege of evoking a poetic memory of a marvellous trip, many years after we have left it.

NEAR VITORIA.

INDEX OF PROPER NAMES

People's names are printed in italics. The numbers in heavy type refer to the illustrations.

SMALL GLOSSARY OF ART TERMS

Altar mayor : High altar.

Artesonado : Coffered ceiling.

Ayuntamiento : Town hall.

Azulejos : Ceramic tiles in several colours.

Bodegon : Still life in painting.

Camarin : Chapel where a statue or holy picture is kept.

Capilla Mayor : Equivalent of the choir in French cathedrals because of its location : the *altar mayor* stands here.

Cimborio : Lantern-tower in a church.

Coro : In Spain the canons' choir or *coro* is enclosed within the bays of the nave that are nearest to the transept. In some convents, it is over the main door ; then it is called the *coro alto*.

Crucero : Transept.

Plaza Mayor : Main square.

Paseo : Public walk.

Paso : Chariot on which statues or groups of statues of Christ, the Virgin and the figures of the Passion are paraded during Holy Week.

Silleria : Group of stalls in the *coro*.

Trasaltar : Back part of the enclosure of the *coro*, fitted with an altar.

Trascoro : Front of this enclosure.